LORRAINE PASCALE

HOW TO BE
A BETTER
COOK

LORRAINE PASCALE

HOW TO BE A BETTER COOK

Harper
Collins

First published by HarperCollins*Publishers* 2014

HarperCollins*Publishers*
77–85 Fulham Palace Road,
Hammersmith, London W6 8JB
www.harpercollins.co.uk

10 9 8 7 6 5 4 3 2 1

A catalogue record of this book is available from the
British Library

ISBN: 978-0-00-748968-8

Food styling: Annie Rigg and Joanna Farrow (Cover)
Props styling: Tony Hutchinson

Printed and bound in Italy by L.E.G.O S.p.A

Devised and presented by Lorraine Pascale and
produced by BBC Bristol

MIX
Paper from
responsible sources
FSC
www.fsc.org
FSC® C007454

INTRODUCTION

It's never too late to learn to cook. I am living proof! I didn't start cooking until I was in my thirties. And now I've taught absolute beginners to make some tasty, impressive dishes in one day. They've gone from only being able to boil an egg (just!) to working on a street food stall. Anybody can cook – and I mean anybody. It just takes some enthusiasm and a little practice.

So if you've always wanted to be able to entertain friends and treat them to a delicious celebration meal or you just want to rely less on ready-meals in your day-to-day family life, this book is designed for you. Before you know it, you'll be dishing up delicious, simple meals with confidence.

The first thing you need to learn is my mantra: 'It's all fine!' That's the secret weapon. It's all in your attitude. If you can relax and just take it easy, you'll be fine. Learning to cook is a process and you might make some mistakes along the way, but you'll learn some lessons and maybe even improvise.

My hope is that after playing around with the recipes, you'll start to trust your palate. You'll even be able to do a bit of freestyling: experimenting with spices and playing with the balance of heat and cool in your dishes. I don't want you to be scared to add a bit of chilli. You'll learn that you don't need to be TOO exact. The ribs recipe, for example, is delicious even if you add a little more or a little less of this or that.

In this book I took on an experiment, too. My family and I were bored with the usual roast chicken so I decided to mix it up and try roast chicken every way I could imagine from Tandoori Roast Chicken to Whole Roast Thai Green Curry Chicken. We still can't decide which of the five kinds in this book we like best! But it was a fun experiment and that's what I want to inspire you to try at home.

And most important of all, I hope you'll learn to trust your own palate, to really taste the food and play around to make a meal just right for you and whoever you are cooking for. If you're cooking for kids, you might want a little less of a chilli kick; if you're making a meal for adults who have grown up with power-packed spicy dishes, maybe you want to turn up the heat. I hope you'll become more sensitive to the balance of flavours – sweet with salty whether ≫

you're creating your very own signature cocktail or making a curry. And once you get the right mix of flavours, you can also start to consider the texture (the crunchiness of red pepper against the softness of avocado in a salsa) for dishes that intrigue and delight.

I'll demystify the art of baking and inspire you to get your mixing bowls out, even if you've never baked a cake in your life! I'll show you how to dress up a simple sponge with fruit and chocolate: you can choose white or dark, berries or mango. And you'll start to see that it's not rocket science.

Let me say it simply: cooking is just putting food together in the right way, the right order and the right amounts! That's all there is to it. The classic newbie expects cooking to be more complicated than it is. But once you roll your sleeves up and get stuck in, you'll start to relax and the kitchen will become a fun family place to be.

And cooking isn't just an idle pastime. Mealtimes bring people together, whether it's busy weekday suppers to nourish your family or celebrations to mark special milestones. Eating and sharing food is a necessary daily ritual, so we might as well make the most of it: dazzling our palates, having fun creating menus, getting your guests – and kids – involved in the prep.

To help you really get started, I've also collected my favourite tips, which are scattered throughout the book, and a few handy tricks at the end. I'm letting you in on all my tried-and-true kitchen secrets – from how to produce the perfect poached egg every time, which can be very impressive perched atop my asparagus starter, to little life-saving cheats so that you never have a cheesecake that cracks down the middle again.

Best of all, I've included a recipe I invented by complete accident – my secret meringue trick! One time when I was in a hurry, I started to put the ingredients in the bowl in the wrong order, but the meringues turned out better than ever. Now I follow that method every time. I hope you'll believe me when I say that mistakes can be the best way of learning sometimes, so get cooking and, above all, have some fun. Indulge your senses and adjust the seasoning to satisfy your palate, and then add more crunch if that's what you like. It's your kitchen, your food!
The biggest secret of all is that being a better cook is just about trusting yourself! You can do it!

Lorraine x

CANAPES &
COCKTAILS

ROASTED 'RAJUN CAJUN' CASHEWS

MAKES
500g

2 tsp sunflower oil
1 egg white
2 tsp paprika
2 tsp cayenne pepper
Leaves from 6 sprigs of fresh
   thyme, finely chopped
   (to give about 4 tsp)
400g raw cashew nuts
100g blanched almonds
Flaked sea salt and freshly ground
   black pepper

Whilst I do not profess to be one of the Cajun cooking cognoscenti, I can claim to have a big love of Cajun fiery food. Sadly, my only visit to New Orleans, where the restaurants and streets are bursting full of fun and flavour, was when I was a young twenty-something model. Not really thinking about food at the time, I was more inclined to dine on salads (no dressing) and possibly, as a treat, a steamed piece of fish. Needless to say, I missed out on so many wonderful foods. I have since done lots of catching up and hope you enjoy my take on these southern American-style tasty cashew nuts.

Preheat the oven to 200°C, (fan 180°C), 400°F, Gas Mark 6. Brush a large baking tray with the oil.

Put the egg white in a large bowl with the paprika, cayenne pepper, 3 teaspoons of the thyme, a pinch of salt and a few twists of black pepper. Whisk up a little and then tip the nuts in, giving them a good stir to make sure everything is nicely covered. Tip them onto the baking tray, arrange in a single layer and bake in the oven for 10–12 minutes, tossing them about halfway through. They should just be catching colour and be rich and shiny.

Once cooked, remove from the oven and leave for a few minutes until cool enough to handle. Then, while still warm, toss the remaining teaspoon of thyme through and season with a little more salt, if necessary.

Tip the nuts into a bowl and serve whilst still a bit warm. They are just as delicious served at room temperature, but pass them back through the oven for a few minutes to warm up again for serving, if preferred.

These can be prepared up to a week ahead of time and stored in an airtight container once cool.

Top tip
The nuts are also delicious served with a tablespoon of honey drizzled over them and tossed through.

CUCUMBER AND FETA BITES WITH DILL AND POMEGRANATE

1 cucumber
75g feta cheese, drained
1 tbsp fresh dill, finely chopped
½ tsp freshly ground black pepper
3 tbsp pomegranate seeds

MAKES
16–18 bites

Whenever there is a party and little canapés are being handed around, they are usually yummy morsels of cheese, sticky sausages and other delicious comfort food fare. I wanted to come up with something that was lighter on the tum than the traditional bite-sized treats, but still wanted lots of flavour, texture and colour. These cucumber bites are really rather tasty. And if you are not entertaining any time soon, try these flavours in a salad using a base of spinach or pea shoots instead.

Top, tail and then peel the cucumber. Cut into 1.5–2cm thick slices to give about 16 to 18 in total. Using a melon baller, small teaspoon or a ½ teaspoon measuring spoon, scoop out enough of the seeds from the middle to give a cup that has a border about 5mm thick, making sure you don't go right down to the bottom. Arrange them on a large platter and set aside.

Break the feta cheese into a small bowl and mash it with a fork until as smooth as possible. Add the dill and season it with the pepper (but no salt as feta is already salty), stirring everything together well. Divide the feta cheese mixture into the cucumber cups. Arrange a little pile of pomegranate seeds on top of each one and serve.

SCARY 'MUMMY' SAUSAGE ROLLS

MAKES
12 using sausages
or 15 using chipolatas

These sausage rolls are really for the children, but if you are a big kid like me, then they will be an awesome centrepiece for your Halloween party. I find ready rolled pastry quick and convenient to use, but you can use a block of pastry of the equivalent weight if preferred. Just roll it out on a lightly floured surface into a 23 x 38cm rectangle, about the thickness of a quarter of a £1 coin.

2 tsp sunflower oil
12 sausages or 15 chipolatas
320g ready rolled puff pastry
1 beaten egg, to glaze
75g American mustard

Heat the oil in a large frying pan over a low heat and gently fry the sausages or chipolatas for about 8 minutes, turning often, until lightly browned all over. Transfer to a plate and leave for about 20 minutes until cool.

After this time, preheat the oven to 220°C, (fan 200°C), 425°F, Gas Mark 7.

Unroll the ready rolled pastry, leaving it sitting on its plastic wrapping. The pastry should be about 38cm long and 23cm wide (or trim with a knife or roll to this size with a rolling pin if not far off). Using a long knife or pastry cutter, cut out 38 x 1cm wide strips across the width (so they will be about 23cm long).

Now, simply wrap the strips around the cooled sausages or chipolatas like mummies' bandages, leaving a gap near one end for the mummies' eyes to go on later. Use three strips per sausage or two and a half strips per chipolata. There will be the odd bit left over, but just add them onto a sausage or chipolata to use them up. Don't worry if the pastry strips stretch or break as you wrap, just patch it up and keep wrapping. The mummies are best looking rustic anyhow. Place them down on a baking tray as you go, eye side up. If at any time you find the pastry is getting too soft, then pop it in the fridge for 10 minutes or until firmed up.

Once all wrapped, brush the pastry with the beaten egg. Place them in the oven to cook for about 20 minutes or until the pastry is golden brown and the sausages are fully cooked through. Transfer to a serving platter. Using the end of a teaspoon, place two dots of mustard on the exposed sausage of each one to create eyes. Serve at once with the remaining mustard for dipping.

PRAWN, PROSCIUTTO AND ROSEMARY SKEWERS WITH AVOCADO, GINGER AND LIME SALSA

SERVES
4

I had planned to do a prawn cocktail, but could not get it to look pretty enough, so I started to thread prawns onto rosemary skewers rather than wooden and was quite happy with the way they turned out. To add some extra flavour to this, the salsa really packs a lively punch.

PRAWN, PROSCIUTTO AND ROSEMARY SKEWERS

2 slices of prosciutto
16 sustainably caught raw peeled jumbo king prawns, de-veined (defrosted if frozen)
8 stalks of fresh rosemary, leaves removed from all but the top of each stalk
1 tbsp olive oil
Lemon wedges, to serve

AVOCADO, GINGER AND LIME SALSA

2 perfectly ripe avocados, peeled, de-stoned and sliced
2 limes (1 quartered, the other juiced)
2 large tomatoes, deseeded and diced into 1cm pieces
5 spring onions, trimmed and finely sliced
1–2 red chillies, deseeded for less heat if preferred, very finely diced
3cm piece of fresh ginger, peeled and finely chopped
1 tbsp olive oil
1 small bunch of either fresh coriander or basil, roughly torn or chopped (to give about 2 tbsp in total)
Flaked sea salt and freshly ground black pepper

First, prepare the salsa. Toss the avocado slices gently in a bowl with the lime juice. Then add the tomato, spring onion, chilli, ginger and olive oil. Reserve a small handful of coriander (or basil) leaves for garnishing, then add the rest to the bowl with salt and pepper, to taste. I like to stir everything together gently to keep the avocados from going too mushy, to give a salsa rather than a guacamole-type consistency. Cover with cling film and pop in the fridge whilst you get on with the skewers.

Cut the prosciutto slices across the width to give four even-sized strips for each one, and then in half lengthways to give sixteen pieces in total, one for each prawn. Wrap each piece of prosciutto around the centre of each prawn like a blanket. Make a prawn into a 'C' shape and push the bottom end of a rosemary stalk in through the top of the 'C' and right through to the bottom. Push the prawn up the stalk to the leaves and then add another prawn in the same way. Repeat to make eight skewers in total. If the rosemary stalk is not easy to push through, then just get a skewer and push that through first to make the holes, then pull it out and push the prawns on.

Get a griddle or frying pan nice and hot. Brush the prawns with a little oil, season and then, working in batches if necessary, griddle them for 1–2 minutes each side, depending on their size, until cooked through. Keep each batch on a warm plate covered with tin foil as you cook the next.

Once all the prawns are cooked, divide the salsa among four serving plates. Sit two prawn skewers on top and add a lime wedge for squeezing to each one. Garnish with the reserved coriander (or basil) leaves and serve.

BAKED ROSEMARY COURGETTE FRITTERS SERVED WITH MARINARA SAUCE DIP AND ROASTED GARLIC SKINNY DIP

SERVES
6

I remember back in the 70s when everyone would make chips by hand. Peel them, chop them and then stick them in the oil and fry 'em. And then came the oven chip, bagged and ready-to-go to make the job much easier. Throughout the journey of the homemade chip to the oven chip, I have developed a strong love affair with the chip. I am under no illusions, however, that you could stick these on a plate next to some cod, serve them to the family and pretend like nothing has happened. But as something a bit different and to add variety to your dishes, these baked courgette fritters are really rather good, and I even got the kiddies to eat them without so much as a whisper of a complaint.

ROASTED GARLIC SKINNY DIP
1 tsp extra virgin olive oil
1 large bulb of garlic, with the top sliced off
200g low-fat cream cheese
3 tbsp low-fat Greek yogurt
½ bunch of chives, finely chopped

MARINARA SAUCE DIP
2 tbsp olive oil
1 large red onion, finely chopped
2 garlic cloves, finely chopped
400g tin of chopped tomatoes
Leaves from 2 sprigs of fresh thyme, finely chopped (to give about 1 tsp)
Pinch of caster sugar (optional)
Large handful of fresh basil leaves, roughly torn

ROSEMARY COURGETTE FRITTERS
3 medium eggs
50g wholemeal or plain flour
125g dried natural breadcrumbs
Flaked sea salt and freshly ground black pepper
2 packed tbsp finely grated Parmesan cheese
Leaves from 2 stalks of fresh rosemary, finely chopped (to give about 2 tsp)
2 medium courgettes (as straight as possible)
Spray oil

TO SERVE
1 small lemon, cut into wedges

Firstly, to make the roasted garlic skinny dip, preheat the oven to 220°C, (fan 200°C), 425°F, Gas Mark 7. Drizzle the oil in the centre of a 20cm square of tin foil and sit the garlic, cut side down, on top. Wrap up loosely, sit on a small baking tray and pop in the oven straight away to cook for about 50–55 minutes or until very soft.

Meanwhile, prepare the marinara sauce. Heat the oil in a medium pan over a low heat. Add the onion and cook for 6–8 minutes until beginning to soften, stirring regularly. Add the garlic and cook for a further minute. Then stir in the tomatoes, thyme, sugar (if you think it needs a little sweetening) and some salt and pepper. Turn down the heat so that the mixture is just simmering and leave to cook for 15–20 minutes or until the sauce has thickened and the flavours have intensified.

Meanwhile, make the courgette fritters. Line two large baking trays with baking parchment. Beat the eggs in a large shallow bowl. Put the flour into another bowl and stir in a couple of large pinches of salt and lots of pepper. Divide the breadcrumbs, Parmesan and rosemary evenly between two large shallow bowls and set all aside.

Trim the courgette ends and slice one lengthways into three even-sized slices. Cut each slice into three long, even-sized strips and then in half across their width to give eighteen chips. Repeat with the second courgette to give thirty-six chips in total. Each one will be 1.5cm wide x 7–8cm long, depending on the size of your courgettes. ≫

BAKED ROSEMARY COURGETTE FRITTERS SERVED WITH MARINARA SAUCE DIP AND ROASTED GARLIC SKINNY DIP

(continued)

Working with a few at a time, toss the batons in the flour until well coated. This will help the egg to stick at the next stage. Toss the batons through the beaten egg and after allowing the excess egg to drip off, roll them around in one of the batches of breadcrumbs to stick all over evenly. Arrange in a single layer on the baking trays as you go. Repeat until all of the courgettes are coated, using the second batch of breadcrumbs once the first has been used up. I like to use a fresh batch of crumbs halfway through as they tend to become too clumpy and sticky to work with. This is quite fiddly and fun (and messy) and is a great way to get children involved in cooking.

The marinara sauce will probably be nice and thick at this stage. If it is too thick to pour, stir in a little water. Remove from the heat, season to taste with salt and pepper, add the torn basil leaves and cover to keep warm until ready to serve.

Spray the courgettes with the oil and place in the oven (with the roasting garlic). If tight on space, nestle the garlic parcel onto one of the courgette trays. Halfway through the cooking time, remove the courgettes, turn them over, give another spray and pop them back in the oven, this time on the opposite shelves to those they were already on. When cooked they should be lightly browned and very crisp all over.

Once softened, remove the garlic from the oven and, when cool enough to handle, unwrap it and squeeze the garlic from their papery jackets into a medium bowl. Mash it lightly with a fork and then add the cream cheese, yogurt and chives and stir everything together really well. Season to taste and spoon into a serving bowl.

Spoon the marinara sauce into a serving bowl. Pile the courgettes onto a serving platter and serve with the two dips and the lemon wedges.

SALT-AND-PEPPER SZECHUAN PRAWNS WITH SOY CHILLI DIPPING SAUCE

SERVES
4

There is a restaurant near me that serves the most enticing Chinese food. I have become a bit of a regular there due to my addiction to their salt-and-pepper squid, which is great for my tum, but not so great for the bank balance. I decided I must take inspiration from this marvelled culinary eating establishment and make up my own, slightly healthier version, and this is the result. It has fast become the number one most requested fish dish in my family now.

SZECHUAN PRAWNS
½ tsp Szechuan pepper
2 tsp five-spice powder
40 sustainably caught raw peeled tiger prawns, de-veined
1 tsp sunflower oil
Flaked sea salt

SOY CHILLI DIPPING SAUCE
5 tbsp mirin (found in my supermarket with the Chinese ingredients)
4 tbsp dark soy sauce
1 tsp soft light brown sugar
1 red chilli, deseeded for less heat if preferred, finely sliced
1 green chilli, deseeded for less heat if preferred, finely sliced

TO GARNISH
1 small spring onion
1 small red chilli

First, prepare the garnishes. Trim and cut the spring onion in half and then cut each piece into really thin lengthways strips. Pop them into a small bowl of iced water, cover and sit in the freezer until ready to serve. Halve the chilli lengthways, deseed and then slice it into long, thin strips. Again, pop into a bowl of iced water and keep covered in the freezer until serving.

To make the sauce, simply stir everything together in a small bowl. Pour into a nice serving bowl and set aside.

Now, for the prawns. Using a pestle and mortar, grind up the Szechuan pepper with a pinch of salt until fairly smooth. Tip this mixture into a small, dry wok, add the five-spice and toast over a low to medium heat for 1–2 minutes, stirring regularly until you start to smell the spices. Tip the spices into a medium bowl and toss the prawns through to coat evenly.

Return the wok to a high heat and add the oil. Stir-fry the spice-coated prawns for 2 minutes until pink throughout. Sit the bowl of dipping sauce on one side of a serving plate (for sharing) and spoon the prawns beside. Drain the spring onion and chilli garnishes from the iced water. They should now have curled nicely. Scatter them over the prawns to garnish and serve at once.

Top tip
To de-vein the prawns, hold the prawns with the back facing upwards. Using a small knife, cut along the length of the back, about 5mm deep. This should expose the black vein. Using either your fingers or the tip of the knife, lift the entire vein out and discard.

SIMPLE TORTILLA PIZZA BITES WITH TOMATOES, PECORINO CHEESE AND ROCKET

SERVES
4

I have said many times over that I often have a frozen pizza in the fridge for those kinds of emergencies when I am really not in the mood to cook. They serve a purpose for sure. But at other times, when I fancy making a cheat's pizza, then these tasty tortilla pizza bites do just the trick.

Spray oil
4 x 19cm wholemeal or white soft flour or corn tortillas
1 small garlic clove, peeled and halved
400g tin of chopped tomatoes (preferably the one with herbs)
½–¼ tsp chilli flakes (optional)
125g pecorino cheese (or a mature Cheddar), coarsely grated
285g jar roasted red and yellow peppers, drained (to give about 175g peppers)
70g bag of rocket
Small handful of fresh basil leaves (optional)
2–3 tsp balsamic vinegar (optional)
2–3 tsp extra virgin olive oil (optional)
Flaked sea salt and freshly ground black pepper

Turn the oven on as high as it will go, making sure two shelves are set in place. Mine goes to 240°C, (fan 220°C), 450°F, Gas Mark 8. Spray a bit of oil on two large baking sheets and place two tortillas down on each of them. Spray a little more on top of the tortillas and then rub the cut side of the garlic all over the tortillas. This gives the pizzas a little extra splash of flavour.

Divide the chopped tomatoes evenly among the four tortillas, spreading them out but leaving a 1.5cm border. Scatter over the chilli, if using, and divide the cheese and peppers evenly over the tops also. Pop both trays into the oven to bake for about 4–6 minutes (depending on how hot your oven is) until the cheese has melted and the tortillas become crisp and golden on their edges. Swap the trays around on the shelves halfway through for even cooking.

Remove them from the oven and slide one onto each serving plate. Top with the rocket and basil, if using. Season with a little scattering of salt and pepper, then drizzle with balsamic vinegar and some extra virgin olive oil, if you fancy it.

QUICK STICKY HONEY AND CHIVE SAUSAGES

SERVES
6–8

I rarely go out to paint the town red, but when I do go to an 'event' the most important thing about the catering for me is not the drinks and cocktails but the canapés. This is my all-time favourite canapé, really quick and easy to do at home and totally and utterly moreish.

1 tbsp sunflower oil
400g pack of uncooked cocktail sausages (about 30 sausages)
4 squidges of honey
½ pack of fresh chives, very finely chopped (to give about 2 tbsp)
Freshly ground black pepper

Drizzle the oil into a large frying pan and place on a medium to high heat. Snip the sausages apart with a scissors, if necessary, and add them to the pan along with some pepper (but not salt as the sausages will most likely be quite salty). Cook for about 5–6 minutes, tossing them about the pan regularly to ensure even cooking. They are done when they are cooked through and piping hot in the centre.

Once cooked, tip the sausages into a colander set over a bowl and allow the excess fat to drain off. Wipe the pan out with kitchen towel and return it to the heat. Toss the sausages back in and stir the honey through, allowing them to cook for a further minute so the honey melts. Remove from the heat, toss the chives through and pile the sausages into a serving dish. Serve at once with cocktail sticks for people to pick them up with.

CHORIZO AND LEMONGRASS PUFF PASTRY SCROLLS

MAKES
32

For those of you who are not yet super comfortable in the kitchen, but want to start getting into making something special, these little scrolls are a great start. So simple to do but the end result has a great impact. Weird, but it works.

Plain flour, for dusting
340g puff pastry (not ready rolled as it usually breaks up when you open it)
18 slices of chorizo (about 7cm wide)
1 stick of lemongrass
1 egg, lightly beaten
Freshly ground black pepper

Line a large baking tray with baking parchment and set aside.

Lightly dust a clean work surface with flour and roll the pastry out to a 25 x 35cm rectangle.

Arrange six chorizo slices in a slightly overlapping layer in a row down one long side. Repeat to give three rows in total, which completely cover the pastry.

Top and tail the lemongrass stick and then remove the one or two outer layers. Slice the stick very thinly and then sprinkle this evenly over the chorizo. Season with a little twist of pepper.

With the longest side facing you, roll up the pastry away from you, really tightly like a Swiss roll, to be about 4cm thick. Carefully lift onto the baking tray and then pop it into the fridge to firm up for about 20 minutes.

Preheat the oven to 220°C, (fan 200°C), 425°F, Gas Mark 7.

Once the pastry is nice and firm, use a sharp knife to cut the 'roll' into 32 slices, each about 1cm thick. Lay each one down on the baking tray, spaced apart, as you go. Brush the sides facing upwards with the beaten egg.

Bake in the oven for 15–20 minutes or until the pastry has puffed up and turned a good golden brown. Once baked, remove from the oven, leave to cool for a couple of minutes and then serve on a party platter!

Top tip
Change up the fillings if you fancy it, using things like sundried tomatoes and thyme or cheese and spring onions.

PEANUT SOUP SHOTS

MAKES
1 litre (20 x 50ml shot glass servings)

These are nice served hot and lovely served at room temperature or cool. Totally and utterly scrummy. If you can find some lovely shot glasses, these make a really, really tasty starter as the soup is quite brown looking and the art of serving this up will all be in the presentation. I based these peanut shots on an African peanut stew, which they serve, I believe, in Ghana, West Africa, amongst other places.

1 tbsp sunflower oil
1 large red onion, finely chopped
3 garlic cloves, finely chopped
3cm piece of fresh ginger, peeled and very finely chopped
1 litre chicken or vegetable stock
150g smooth peanut butter (no added sugar)
150g tinned chopped tomatoes
2–3 red chillies, deseeded for less heat if preferred, finely diced
Juice of 2 limes

25g salted, roasted (not dry-roasted) peanuts, finely chopped (optional)
Flaked sea salt and freshly ground black pepper

EQUIPMENT
20 x 50ml shot glasses

Heat the oil in a large pan over a low to medium heat. Add the onion and cook for 10 minutes or so, stirring occasionally, until softened and just starting to colour. Add the garlic and ginger and cook for 1 more minute.

Increase the heat to medium to high, add the chicken or vegetable stock and bring to the boil. Then add the peanut butter, tinned tomatoes and chillies (using however many you dare). Bring back to the boil and let it bubble away for 5 minutes to thicken slightly. Add the lime juice, then remove from the heat and season to taste with salt and pepper.

If you would like the soup to be completely smooth, then blitz it with a blender. I prefer it like this. Pour into 20 x 50ml shot glasses. Top with the roasted peanuts, if liked, and serve.

LYCHEE, BASIL AND MINT BELLINI

SERVES
1

There are two ways of making this refreshing drink and I have included both here. The first one has the lychees bobbing about in the liquid, which some may think looks akin to something you might find in an old doctor's surgery (I will leave that to your imagination!). In the other method, the lychees are blended in with the drink to give much more flavour and ease of drinking, so the choice is up to you.

2 lychees (from a tin)
1 tbsp lychee juice
 (from the tin also)
125ml Prosecco, cava, sparkling
 wine, Champagne (or lemonade
 for a non-alcoholic version),
 well chilled
2–3 fresh mint leaves
2–3 fresh basil leaves

Pop the lychees and lychee juice into a 200ml champagne flute (or other tall glass).

Slowly pour in your choice of bubbly to come almost to the top.

Rip the mint and basil leaves on top and serve at once.

BLENDED VERSION

4 lychees (from a tin)
2 tbsp lychee juice
 (from the tin also)
125ml Prosecco, cava, sparkling
 wine, Champagne (or lemonade
 for a non-alcoholic version),
 well chilled
2-3 fresh mint leaves
2-3 fresh basil leaves

Blitz the lychees with 2 tablespoons of juice from the tin with a mini or stick blender until smooth. Pour into a 200ml champagne flute (or other tall glass).

Slowly pour in your choice of bubbly to come almost to the rim, then rip the mint and basil leaves over the top and serve at once.

WHITE 'SANGRIA'

SERVES
6–8

4 tbsp caster sugar
700ml bottle Rioja white wine
200ml brandy
2 large handfuls of ice
250g mango slices or cubes
   (from 1 medium mango
   or ready-prepared)
2 peaches, cut into eighths
2 limes, sliced
Large handful of fresh basil leaves
Large handful of fresh mint leaves
500–700ml soda water

In early January 2014, the favourite drink of the English when visiting Portugal or Spain was given protected EU status, meaning that sangria on a label can only be called sangria if it has been made in Portugal or Spain. The name sangria means 'blood letting' as traditionally sangria is made with red wine. I hope the Spanish and the Portuguese will forgive me when I propose to you a white version, which still retains the traditional fruitiness, with a touch of brandy for good measure.

Pop the sugar into a small jam jar, add 4 tablespoons cold water and screw the lid on tightly. Then shake the hell out of it for a few minutes until the sugar is completely dissolved.

Pour it into a large serving jug and stir in the wine and brandy. Add the ice, fruit and herbs in layers and then top with soda water, to taste. Serve at once for everyone to share.

FLAVOURED ICE CUBES

I have given these ideas here for flavoured ice cubes, but you can obviously use whatever fruit you have knocking about. These look great loaded up in a glass jug with fresh fruit for an extra quaffable and dramatic effect.

EQUIPMENT
One ice-cube tray with 12 holes (each hole in mine holds about 20ml liquid, which is about average)

WHEN LIFE GIVES YOU LEMONS

Zest and juice of 3 lemons

Divide the lemon juice among the 12 holes in the tray. Put the zest of quarter of a lemon in each ice cube hole. Top with water and freeze until set.

COOL AS A CUCUMBER

½ cucumber, peeled if preferred, cut into 6 slices, then cut in quarters
12 small fresh mint sprigs

Put two cucumber quarters and a mint sprig into each ice cube hole. Top with water and then freeze until set.

IN THE LIMELIGHT

1 lime, cut into 6 slices, then cut in half
4 sprigs of fresh thyme, each sprig cut into 3

Place one piece of lime and a sprig of thyme into each hole in an ice-cube tray. Fill each one with water and freeze until set.

HIBISCUS

6 hibiscus flowers in syrup, halved (I bought mine online)
4 tbsp syrup from the hibiscus jar

Pop a hibiscus flower half into each ice-cube tray hole. Divide the syrup among the holes and then top with water. Freeze until set.

EARN YOUR STRIPES

250ml pomegranate juice

Pour 2 teaspoons of pomegranate juice into each hole of the ice cube tray (each one should be a third full). Pop into the freezer until just set. Remove and put enough water into the ice-cube tray so that the holes are now two-thirds full and pop it back into the freezer to set. Then, divide the remaining pomegranate juice among the ice cube holes and freeze until set.

STRAWBERRY

3 medium-large strawberries, hulled and quartered lengthways

Pop a piece of strawberry in each of the 12 ice-cube tray holes. Top with water and freeze until solid.

RASPBERRY

24 small-medium raspberries

Sit two raspberries in each of the 12 ice-cube tray holes. Top with water and freeze until solid.

IRISH COFFEE WITH A CRÈME CHANTILLY TOPPING

SERVES
4

A coffee cocktail, pimped up with the addition of a rich Chantilly cream topping.

150ml whipping or double cream, cold from the fridge
2 tsp icing sugar
Few drops of vanilla extract or the seeds of ½ a vanilla pod
4 mugs of strong, hot coffee
150ml whisky

Pour the cream into a bowl, sift in the icing sugar and add the vanilla extract or seeds. Whisk the cream until it has just thickened enough to coat the back of a spoon and set it aside for a moment.

I like to serve Irish coffees in thick glasses with a handle and stem, but they will work just fine in a mug. Divide the whisky among the four mugs of hot coffee, stirring them together well.

Take the cream, whisking it up a little more if you think it needs it, and carefully spoon or pour it on top of each of the coffees to give a good 'head'. Serve immediately.

YOU DON'T ALWAYS NEED A PLAN.
SOMETIMES YOU JUST NEED TO BREATHE,
TRUST, LET GO AND SEE WHAT HAPPENS.
MANDY HALE

STARTERS, SNACKS & SOUPS

THAI FISH CAKES WITH A SWEET CHILLI DIPPING SAUCE

MAKES
12

I always order fish cakes when I go out for Thai food. Perfect just after the glass of wine and the whole basket of prawn crackers. When I tested these at home, I managed to eat the whole lot in one fell swoop. I stood at the fridge with the door open eating them one by one, until there were none. Well worth giving these a go.

SWEET CHILLI DIPPING SAUCE
75g caster sugar
25ml rice wine vinegar
1 red chilli, deseeded for less heat if preferred, finely diced
Juice of ½ lime (but zest the lime first as you will need the zest later)

THAI FISH CAKES
250g sustainably caught raw peeled prawns, de-veined and roughly chopped if large
350g sustainably caught skinless fish, like salmon, cod or pollack, bones removed and diced
25g cornflour
4 spring onions, very finely chopped
1 red chilli, deseeded and very finely chopped
1 tbsp green curry paste
Large handful of fresh coriander, stalks and leaves roughly chopped (reserving a few for garnish)
Zest of 1 lime (from the chilli sauce)
Juice of ½ lime
1 tsp caster sugar
About ½ medium egg, beaten
Vegetable oil, for frying
1 lime, quartered, to serve (optional)
Sea salt and freshly ground black pepper

Put the caster sugar, rice wine vinegar, 50ml water and the chilli into a small pan over a low heat and simmer gently, stirring from time to time, until the sugar has dissolved. Turn up the heat and allow it to bubble away for another minute. Then remove from the heat, add the lime juice and pour it into a small serving bowl and set aside.

Blitz the prawns, fish, cornflour, spring onion, chilli, curry paste, coriander, lime zest and juice and sugar in a food processor to a chunky paste. The mixture should have a little texture rather than being smooth. Then tip the mixture into a bowl, stir in the egg and season with salt and pepper.

Shape the mixture into twelve equal-size patties about 5–6cm wide, arranging them on a tray lined with parchment paper as you go. Cover and pop into the fridge while you prepare the oil.

Preheat the oven to 110°C, (fan 100°C), 225°F, Gas Mark ¼.

Put about 1cm of oil into a wide sauté pan and get it nice and hot. You can test the temperature by popping a small square of bread in there. It should gently fry to a nice golden brown in a minute or two and then the oil is perfect. Working in two batches, fry the fish cakes for 3–4 minutes per side until deep golden brown. Be careful as the oil may splatter because of the fish juices. Turn the heat down a little if you think the oil is getting too hot. Drain the fish cakes on kitchen paper and then transfer to a baking tray and keep warm in the oven while cooking the second batch.

Once all are cooked, serve the fish cakes with the sweet chilli sauce and garnish with the reserved coriander. Serve some extra lime wedges to squeeze over the top, if liked.

ASPARAGUS AND EGG PUFF TARTS WITH PARMESAN AND BASIL

SERVES
6

My Achilles heel in cooking has always been poaching eggs. I remember the look on my tutor's face at culinary school when he took a glance at my straggly egg bobbing about in a pan of turbulently boiling water. The white of the egg clung on around the yolk for dear life, leaving strands that found their way around much of the pan. A far simpler method for a perfect poached egg is to have just a little barely bubbling water in a sauté-type pan, then simply slide in the eggs and leave them to cook for a short while. The stiller water and the gentleness of putting them into the water mean that the egg whites stay relatively intact with the yolks, giving you eggs with a perfect poach.

Plain flour, for dusting
1 x 500g packet of puff pastry
200g low-fat cream cheese
Finely grated zest of ¼ lemon
30 medium asparagus spears
Beaten egg (or milk), to glaze
6 medium eggs

TO SERVE
25g Parmesan, made into shavings with a potato peeler
Good handful of small fresh basil leaves
Drizzle of extra virgin olive oil (optional)
Flaked sea salt and freshly ground black pepper

Line a large baking sheet with baking parchment and set aside. Put a little flour out on a clean work surface and then roll out the puff pastry to a 28 x 30cm rectangle and to the thickness of a pound coin, trimming the edges so that the sides are nice and straight and neat. Cut the pastry in half down the length and then into thirds across the width to give six 10 x 14cm rectangles.

Put the pastry rectangles on the baking sheet, cover with cling film and refrigerate for 20 minutes (or pop in the freezer for 10 minutes) for the pastry to firm up. It is important to do this so that when the puff pastry goes into the oven, the flour cooks before the butter melts, ensuring a much lighter pastry.

Preheat the oven to 220°C, (fan 200°C), 425°F, Gas Mark 7.

Mix the cream cheese and lemon zest together in a small bowl and season to taste. Trim the asparagus so that each stem is 10cm long (use the trimmings to make a quick soup or add to a pasta sauce).

Once firm, remove the pastry from the fridge (or freezer) and use a sharp knife to mark a 1cm wide border around each rectangle. Then using a crosshatch pattern, mark the border so each pastry shape looks like a picture frame. Take a fork and prick the centre of each shape about ten times, right through to the baking sheet. Brush the border with the beaten egg (or milk), making sure that it does not go down the sides of the pastry. If this happens, just wipe it away with your finger otherwise the egg will stick the layers of the pastry together and stop the pastry from rising nicely.

Divide the lemony cheese among the six tarts, spreading it out with the back of the spoon and making sure that it stays inside the 'frame'. Lay five asparagus spears in a single layer, touching each other and pointing the same direction on each tart, and push them down slightly.

Bake the tarts in the oven for 18–20 minutes or until the pastry has puffed up nicely and is firm and golden brown where it has risen. ≫

ASPARAGUS AND POACHED EGG PUFF TARTS WITH PARMESAN AND BASIL

(continued)

About 10 minutes before the tarts are ready, pour about 4cm water into a really wide sauté pan or deep frying pan and bring to the boil on a high heat. Then, turn the heat down to bring the water to a gentle simmer. Crack an egg into a very small bowl or tea cup and then slide the egg into the water. Repeat with all of the eggs, spacing them apart. Cook them for 3–4 minutes until the white is cooked, but the yolk is still soft to the touch, and then remove with a slotted spoon onto a warm plate.

Remove the tarts from the oven and divide onto six serving plates. Sit a poached egg on top of each tart and scatter over the Parmesan and basil leaves. Sprinkle with a little salt and pepper and drizzle with a little olive oil, if liked, and serve.

CARIBBEAN TOASTIE CUPS WITH AVOCADO, MANGO AND MINT

MAKES
24

Spray oil

6 x 19cm white, wholemeal or seeded soft flour tortillas (if you use the larger ones, they will need more filling, so I find it best to stick to this size)

1 red pepper, deseeded and cut into 1cm dice

1 ripe but firm avocado, peeled, de-stoned and cut into 1cm dice

1 small ripe mango, peeled and de-stoned or 125g ready-prepared mango cubes, cut into 1cm dice

200g tinned red kidney beans, drained and rinsed

2 spring onions, trimmed and finely sliced

1 red chilli, deseeded for less heat if preferred, finely chopped

Juice of 1 lime

Leaves from ½ a bunch of fresh mint, finely chopped (to give about 2 tbsp)

1 tbsp extra virgin olive oil (optional)

Flaked sea salt and freshly ground black pepper

EQUIPMENT

Two 12-hole shallow (regular) cupcake trays (you can work in two batches if you only have one tray). A muffin tray would work if you used the larger tortillas, but you would need to increase the filling a little

Avocado and mint are not really ingredients that one would think of when dreaming up Caribbean dishes. However, if you go a little bit over to Venezuela, which has a Caribbean coast, avocado is more prolific, which is why I saw fit to add it to this dish. Kidney beans are frequently used in rice and peas (or rice and beans) and are most definitely a Jamaican staple, while the fruity, dribbly rich taste of mango brings all these flavours beautifully together. The toastie cups are a great base for you to continue your journey into cooking. Fill them with fresh fruit, even chilli con carne or your own concoction, for something different every time.

Preheat the oven to 200°C, (fan 180°C), 400°F, Gas Mark 6. Spray the two 12-hole shallow (regular) cupcake trays with oil and set aside.

With the tortillas in a stack on top of one another on a chopping board, cut them into quarters to give twenty-four pieces. Push one quarter into each hole of the cupcake trays, pressing it in to fit. Really press it down to form a sturdy bottom, but the tops should splay out at the top creating a 'cup'. If you find that your tortillas are splitting when you do this, then just pop them in the microwave for 30 seconds to warm up and to make them more pliable.

Pop the tortilla cups in the oven and cook for about 5 minutes until the cups are nice and crisp and brown. Keep an eye on them as they can burn really quickly.

Meanwhile, mix the red pepper, avocado, mango, kidney beans, spring onion, chilli, lime juice and mint together in a large bowl and season to taste. Add a little oil if you like.

Once the tortilla cups are crisp and golden, remove them from the oven and onto a serving plate. Divide the filling mixture evenly among the cups and serve.

These are also delicious with a knob of sour cream served on top of each one.

CHICKEN WRAP WITH GOAT'S CHEESE, CHIVES, SPINACH AND CRANBERRIES

SERVES
2

A lovely quick lunch for those days when you're in a rush. Leftover chicken is great for these wraps, or I often just buy the ready cooked stuff. But if you want to cook the chicken from scratch, then poached or grilled chicken will work nicely.

2 wraps (preferably wholegrain)
75g soft goat's cheese
2 cooked chicken breasts, torn into shreds or cut into thin slices
Large handful of baby spinach leaves
Small handful of dried cranberries
Handful of fresh chives, finely chopped (to give about 1 tsp)
Sea salt and freshly ground black pepper

Lay the wraps on a clean surface and spread each one with half of the goat's cheese. Scatter over the chicken, spinach, cranberries, chives and a little seasoning.

Next, fold up the bottom quarter of a wrap and then roll the wrap over from the left to right to enclose the filling. Wrap the unopened end tightly with baking parchment or cling film to secure and eat!

SMOOTH PUMPKIN AND PARMESAN SOUP

SERVES
6

A very quick and simple soup, especially if you can get the ready-prepared pumpkin/butternut squash cubes to make it!

2 tbsp vegetable or sunflower oil
1 large or 2 medium onions, finely chopped
1.35kg pumpkin (or butternut squash) peeled, deseeded and cut into 2.5cm chunks (to give about 1kg flesh)
2 garlic cloves, finely chopped
750ml vegetable or chicken stock
50g Parmesan cheese, finely grated

TO SERVE
2–3 tbsp double cream (optional)
½ bunch of fresh chives (optional)
Flaked sea salt and freshly ground black pepper

Heat the oil in a large saucepan on a medium heat, add the onion and cook for 5 minutes until softened, but not catching colour. Then add the pumpkin and cook for another 5 minutes. Add the garlic and cook for a further minute before pouring in the stock. Bring it to the boil and then turn down to simmer for about 20 minutes or until the pumpkin is nice and soft.

Once ready, tip in the Parmesan and stir through until it melts, season to taste and then remove the pan from the heat.

Carefully pour the mixture into a blender and blitz it until it is smooth. You may need to work in batches, depending on the size of your blender. Alternatively, blitz in the pan with a stick (or immersion) blender. At this stage you can either just serve it as it is, or sieve it to make it really nice and smooth (in which case it will yield a little less).

Ladle the soup into six serving bowls and serve with a little drizzle of double cream and some chives snipped with scissors, if you fancy.

PUMPKIN, THYME AND CHEDDAR MUFFINS

MAKES
12

These lovely little yummies are a healthy(ish) breakfast snack. Sweet potato works quite well in this recipe too, but the resulting muffin will be a little heavier.

250g pumpkin (or butternut squash), peeled, deseeded and cut into 5mm cubes (to give about 175g flesh)
175g wholemeal flour
100g self-raising flour
1 tbsp fresh thyme leaves, roughly chopped
1 tsp bicarbonate of soda
1 tsp baking powder
Pinch of salt
2 medium eggs
225ml semi-skimmed milk
75ml vegetable oil
150ml natural yogurt
50g mature Cheddar cheese, grated

EQUIPMENT
12-hole muffin tin with paper muffin cases

Preheat the oven to 220°C, (fan 200°C), 425°F, Gas Mark 7. Line a 12-hole muffin tin with paper muffin cases and set aside.

Put the pumpkin, flours, thyme, bicarb, baking powder and salt in a large bowl. Give them a quick stir together and then make a hole in the centre.

Lightly beat the eggs in a medium bowl, then mix in the milk, oil and yogurt until combined. Pour the wet mixture into the centre of the dry ingredients and mix together using as few stirs as possible (otherwise you will make the muffins too dense and heavy). The mixture will be quite wet.

Divide the mixture evenly into the 12 muffin cases. Sprinkle over the grated Cheddar and bake in the centre of the oven for 20–25 minutes or until a skewer inserted in the centre of a muffin comes out clean.

Once cooked, remove from the oven and set aside to cool just a little as these muffins are best eaten warm.

Top tip
The muffins do get a bit stuck to the paper when you are taking them out, but the papers are easier to remove when they are a little cooler.

PROSCIUTTO, PESTO AND MOZZARELLA WRAP

MAKES
2

This classic food combination was brought back to my attention during an invitation to talk at The School of Life near Euston. Here people who want to realise their potential come to listen about ways in which they can follow their dreams and achieve their passions. During the break, a large platter of baguettes chock full of ingredients similar to these were being handed out. So simple but oh, so tasty!

2 wraps (preferably wholegrain)
2 tbsp pesto (shop-bought, or for homemade see page 80)
4 slices of prosciutto
1 handful of rocket (about 25g)
1 large tomato, thinly sliced
125g ball of mozzarella, thinly sliced
Sea salt and freshly ground black pepper

Lay the wraps on a clean surface and spread each one with half of the pesto. Lay the prosciutto over that, followed by a handful of rocket. Lay the tomato and mozzarella slices on top and season with a little salt and pepper.

Next, fold up the bottom quarter of a wrap and then roll the wrap over from the left to right to enclose the filling. Wrap the unopened end tightly with baking parchment or cling film to secure and eat!

BAKED POTATOES WITH CHEESY NACHOS AND SOUR CREAM

SERVES
4

When I was at school down in Devon, they would put on a very impressive bonfire night. We would save our pocket money for weeks on end so we had enough money for the games, gifts and, most importantly, food on offer on the big day. I would always head straight away to the baked potato stand, which would serve hot jackets with way too much butter and a sprinkling of pepper and salt. I have 'pimped' the baked potatoes here, adding some totally scrumptious cheesy nachos, crisp tortilla chips and lashings of sour cream.

4 baking potatoes
150g Cheddar cheese, coarsely grated
200g tin of kidney beans, drained and rinsed
100g cherry tomatoes, quartered (or 100g tomatoes, chopped into chunks)
100g sliced jalapeños (green or red) from a jar, drained (to give about 45g)
1 small red onion, thinly sliced
Leaves from ½ bunch of fresh coriander, roughly chopped

TO SERVE
4 big dollops of sour cream
8 tortilla chips

Preheat the oven to 220°C, (fan 200°C), 425°F, Gas Mark 7.

Prick the potatoes with a fork, arrange on a baking tray and bake in the oven for a good hour or so until a knife inserted into the centre of a potato glides in easily with no give and it's nice and soft inside.

Meanwhile, mix all of the nacho ingredients (reserving some coriander for serving) together and set aside.

Once cooked, use a sharp knife to cut a split line down the centre of each potato, cutting almost all the way through. Open each potato out slightly and divide the nacho filling mixture into them.

Pop back into the oven for about 15 minutes until the cheese melts and the nacho mix is heated through.

Remove from the oven and top each potato with a dollop of sour cream. Put 2 tortilla chips in each potato, scatter the reserved coriander over and serve.

SPICED CHICKPEA FALAFEL WRAPS WITH CUCUMBER AND CORIANDER TZATZIKI

SERVES
2

I am often told by people that they would like simple ideas for lunch. They have had the same things time after time each week and could I come up with something different? The tzatziki gives a lovely freshness to the wrap. I know that coriander is a real no-no for some people, so please swap this for chives or parsley if you prefer.

CUCUMBER AND CORIANDER TZATZIKI
150g Greek yogurt
¼ cucumber, cut into a small dice
Leaves from a small handful of fresh coriander, roughly chopped

SPICED CHICKPEA FALAFELS
2 x 400g tins of chickpeas, drained and rinsed
4 spring onions, finely chopped
2 garlic cloves, finely chopped
2–3 tsp ground cumin
1–2 tsp cayenne pepper (optional)
Leaves from a large handful of fresh coriander
Leaves from a few sprigs of fresh thyme
1 egg, lightly beaten
2 tbsp plain flour
2 tbsp sesame seeds
Sunflower oil

TO SERVE
4 large wholewheat, multigrain or plain flour tortilla wraps
1 small red onion, finely sliced
1 Little Gem lettuce, leaves torn into pieces
1 red chilli, finely sliced (optional)
Flaked sea salt and freshly ground black pepper

Preheat the oven to 200°C, (fan 180°C), 400°F, Gas Mark 6.

Mix the yogurt, cucumber and coriander for the tzatziki together in a small bowl. Season with salt and pepper and then set aside.

Wrap the tortillas well in tin foil and then place them into the oven for about 10 minutes to heat through.

Then for the falafels, put the chickpeas, spring onion, garlic, cumin, cayenne (if using), coriander and thyme, half of the egg (you will only need half an egg for this recipe), the flour and salt and pepper, to taste, in a food processor and blitz together. The mixture should be fairly smooth, but still with a bit of texture.

Divide the mixture into 12 even-sized pieces (each weighing about 50g). Squidge each one into a fairly tight ball so that the mixture stays together well, and then flatten them into roughly 1.5cm thick small patties. Scatter the sesame seeds onto a small plate and gently press both sides of each falafel into them to stick.

Put a little bit of oil in a large frying pan over a medium to high heat and fry the falafels for about 1–2 minutes on each side until they are crisp on the outside and golden brown. Remove them from the pan and leave to cool a little.

Remove the tortillas from the oven and unwrap them. Then spread each one with the tzatziki and scatter over the red onion, lettuce leaves and chilli, if using. Lay three falafels on top of each tortilla and then wrap them up. The falafels can be quite crumbly, but perfect once inside the tortilla.

HARISSA LAMB LOLLIPOPS WITH PEA AND MINT HUMMUS AND LEMON

SERVES
2

I have not included them in the recipe, but these served with some flatbreads really are quite the thing!

PEA AND MINT HUMMUS
1 tbsp olive oil
1 small onion, finely chopped
1 garlic clove, very finely chopped
200g fresh or frozen peas
100g good chicken or vegetable stock (or water)
1 tbsp low-fat Greek yogurt
1 tbsp tahini (I found it in the supermarket – it is a sesame paste)
Leaves from ½ bunch of fresh mint

SESAME DUKKAH
50g sesame seeds
2 tbsp coriander seeds
1 tsp chilli flakes
½ tsp ground cumin
½ tsp ground cinnamon
Pinch of nutmeg

HARISSA LAMB
100g harissa paste (shop-bought, or for homemade see page 79)
6 bone rack of lamb, cut into cutlets
2 tsp olive oil

TO SERVE
Leaves from ½ bunch of fresh mint
1 large lemon, cut into quarters
Flaked sea salt and freshly ground black pepper

Place the oil for the hummus in a medium frying or sauté pan and set over a low to medium heat. Once hot, add the onion and fry for 8–10 minutes, stirring regularly, until well softened.

Meanwhile, put a small frying pan (with no oil in) on a medium heat.

Pop the sesame seeds in and toast for 2–3 minutes until golden. Remove from the heat and tip the sesame seeds into a small bowl. Return the pan to the heat and toast the coriander seeds for 2–3 minutes until fragrant. Remove from the heat and tip into a pestle and mortar. Grind the coriander seeds to a fine powder and add this to the sesame seeds. Toss the remaining dukkah ingredients through the seeds along with a little salt and pepper. Tip onto a large plate and set aside.

Returning to the onion, add the garlic and cook for a further minute, keeping everything moving in the pan so that the garlic does not burn. Add the peas and cook for a minute, then add the stock and cook for a further 3–4 minutes until the peas are cooked. Tip the pea mixture into a blender and leave it to cool down a little.

Meanwhile, set a large griddle or frying pan on a high heat to get it nice and hot. Smear the harissa evenly all over the lamb cutlets, then dip them into the dukkah mix to coat both sides. Drizzle over the oil and place them in the pan to cook for about 3 minutes per side for medium rare (or another minute or two each side if you prefer them more cooked). I like to cook them so they are still nice and moist inside. ≫

HARISSA LAMB LOLLIPOPS WITH PEA AND MINT HUMMUS AND LEMON

(continued)

Meanwhile, return to the hummus and add the yogurt, tahini, mint leaves and a little salt and pepper. Blitz to form a rough paste and set aside.

Once the lamb cutlets are cooked, transfer them to a plate and cover with tin foil. They need to rest for about 5 minutes to allow them to become more succulent and to make sure their juices stay in the meat rather than run out all over the plate.

When ready to serve, spoon the hummus into the centre of each serving plate. Arrange three lamb chops around or on top of each pool of hummus, rip up and scatter over the mint leaves and serve at once with the lemon wedges.

Top tip
Use up any leftover hummus or dukkah as a topping for bruschetta.

BAKED GUILT-FREE KALE CHILLI 'CRISPS'

SERVES
6–8

A crispy, crunchy, tasty, snacky, healthy alternative to regular crisps.

Spray oil
200g kale (or cavolo nero), washed and dried
½ tsp mild chilli powder
Flaked sea salt and freshly ground black pepper

Preheat the oven to 180°C, (fan 160°C), 350°F, Gas Mark 4. Line two large baking trays with baking parchment and spray the parchment with a little oil.

Tear the tough, woody stems from the kale or cavolo nero leaves and discard. Rip each leaf into smaller bite-sized pieces and scatter them in a single layer on each baking tray as you go.

Spritz a little more oil evenly over the kale pieces and then scatter the chilli powder and a good amount of salt and pepper evenly over. Toss each batch around a little to coat and then rearrange them in their single layers.

Bake in the oven for 10 minutes, tossing the leaves halfway through and swapping the trays around on the shelves as you pop them back in. They do burn quite quickly and become bitter, so keep an eye on them. They should be crisp and just becoming darker in colour when ready.

Remove them from the oven, leave for a few minutes until cool enough to handle and then pile into a bowl and serve.

These will keep for a day in an airtight container.

SLOW COOKER LENTIL, SWEET POTATO AND CUMIN SOUP WITH GINGER AND CORIANDER

SERVES
6

The red lentils pair splendidly with the sweet potato in this highly flavoured, aromatic soup. This makes a whole lot of soup, so it is good to freeze some of it, if you like.

1 tbsp cumin seeds
1 tsp coriander seeds, bashed up a bit
2 litres good-quality vegetable or chicken stock
500g dried red lentils
500g sweet potatoes, peeled and diced
1 large onion, finely chopped
1 stick of celery, finely diced
2cm piece of fresh ginger, peeled and finely chopped
1 red chilli, deseeded for less heat if preferred, finely sliced
Leaves from ½ bunch of fresh coriander (or flat-leaf parsley), roughly chopped
Sea salt and freshly ground black pepper

Toast the cumin and coriander seeds in a small dry frying pan over a low to medium heat for 2–3 minutes, shaking occasionally, until becoming fragrant. Tip into a pestle and mortar and grind them roughly, then tip them into a slow cooker along with the remaining ingredients (except the coriander). Pop the lid on and cook on low for 5–6 hours.

Once ready, eat as is or blitz to a smoother consistency with a stick (or immersion) blender, if preferred. If the soup is a bit thick, then thin it out with a little boiling water to your preferred consistency. Season to taste and then serve scattered with coriander (or parsley).

HOMEMADE HARISSA

MAKES
About 200g

1 tbsp cumin seeds
1 tbsp coriander seeds
6 red chillies, roughly chopped
   (if you are serious about harissa,
   you will leave the seeds in!)
4 garlic cloves, roughly chopped
6 tbsp extra virgin olive oil
1 tbsp tomato purée
1 tbsp cayenne pepper
Leaves from 1 bunch of
   fresh coriander
Flaked sea salt and freshly ground
   black pepper

My name is Lorraine and I am a harissa junky. I use it on so many things from sandwiches to pastas to roasts. The stuff in the pot that you can buy is great, but homemade is a wonderful thing too, if you have the time.

Toast the cumin and coriander seeds in a small frying pan (with no oil in it) over a medium to high heat for about 2–3 minutes or until you can start to smell the heady aromas.

Tip the seeds into the bowl of a mini blender and add the remaining ingredients. Blend the mixture to form a paste. Season with a little salt and pepper and then pop in a jar with a tight-fitting lid until ready to use.

This will keep in the fridge for up to a week.

Top tip
I know toasting the spices is a mini faff, but it's a hugely flavour-enhancing step and really makes a monumental difference to the finished dish.

PACIFIC PESTO

I had this unusual pesto in Australia in Byron Bay. There is a fish shop just off the main street and near the beach. They serve the best, best fish. Not all battered, just fresh grilled with salad, some chippies, as they call them, and some pesto. I had to try to get the recipe, which they would not give me, so I have gallantly attempted here to make that very same pesto.

Leaves from 1 bunch of fresh basil (to give about 4 tbsp)
Leaves from 1 bunch of fresh coriander (to give about 15–20g)
2 garlic cloves, roughly chopped
75ml extra virgin olive oil
3 tbsp sweet chilli sauce
Sea salt and freshly ground black pepper

Blitz all of the ingredients together using a stick (or immersion) blender or jug blender. Season to taste and then it is ready to use.

This pesto can be stored in a container with a tight-fitting lid in the fridge for up to a week.

STARTING IS HALF THE BATTLE.

SALADS

ROASTED DUCK AND WATERMELON SALAD WITH TOASTED CASHEW NUTS

SERVES
4

This dish has become a favourite in many of the Asian restaurants that I go to in London. I always order this when I see it on the menu. And this is my own version. Now watermelon is not something you see every day in the shops, but more so in the summer. So when you see one, reach out and grab it (or the stuff that is pre-prepared) as this little salad is bloomin' lovely!

2 x 250g duck breasts
1 tsp five-spice powder
100g plain cashew nuts
　(not salted or roasted)
250g watermelon (about ¼ of
　a small one), skin and seeds
　removed, flesh cut into cubes
1 bunch of spring onions, trimmed
　and cut on the diagonal
1 red chilli, finely sliced
Leaves from 1 bunch of fresh mint
　(to give 4 tbsp)
Leaves from ½ bunch of fresh
　coriander or ½ bunch of
　fresh basil (to give 2 tbsp)
Sea salt and freshly ground
　black pepper

DRESSING
4 tbsp soy sauce
Finely grated zest and juice
　of 1 lime
1 tsp sesame oil
2cm piece of fresh ginger,
　peeled and very finely diced
1 garlic clove, finely grated
1 tsp caster sugar

Preheat the oven to 200°C, (fan 180°C), 400°F, Gas Mark 6.

Using a long, sharp knife, score the skin on the duck breasts in a crisscross pattern. Rub the five-spice all over the breasts to evenly coat and then season them well with salt and pepper. Put the breasts skin-side down into a medium (ovenproof if you have one) frying pan. Place the pan on a medium heat and cook for about 8 minutes, without moving them, until the skin is crisp and golden and the fat has rendered.

Meanwhile, heat a small dry frying pan on a low heat and toast the cashew nuts for a few minutes, tossing regularly, until golden. Remove, tip them into a large bowl and leave to cool.

Once the duck breasts are ready, turn them over so they are skin-side up, drain off the fat and transfer the pan to the oven. If your pan doesn't fit or is not ovenproof, then transfer the duck breasts into a small roasting tin. Cook them for 10 minutes for a pink finish (or another 5 minutes if you prefer them cooked through).

Meanwhile, mix together the dressing ingredients in a mug with a fork and set them aside to infuse. Toss the watermelon into the bowl with the cashews and add the spring onion, chilli, mint and coriander or basil and set aside.

Once the duck breasts are cooked, remove from the oven and leave to rest and cool for 5 minutes. Then, halve them down their length and cut each piece into thin slices. Toss the duck through the salad along with the dressing until well mixed. Serve at once.

Top tip
Scoring the skin before cooking helps the fat to render (melt) out and make the skin nice and crispy.

GRILLED PEACH, BURRATA AND BASIL SALAD WITH A DIJON DRESSING

SERVES
4

Parma ham would be a nice addition to this if you fancied it. Burrata is becoming increasingly popular in restaurants and is a very, very delicious thing. Take mozzarella cream and then wrap it in more mozzarella and then you have burrata. An insanely decadent cheese.

DIJON DRESSING
3 tbsp extra virgin olive oil
1 tbsp balsamic vinegar (not a syrupy one)
1 tsp Dijon mustard

GRILLED PEACHES
2 tsp olive oil
4 peaches, almost ripe but not too soft, quartered and stoned

TO SERVE
2 x 125g balls of mozzarella or 200g ball of burrata, drained and torn into chunks
70g bag of rocket
Leaves from 1 bunch of fresh basil, roughly torn
Flaked sea salt and freshly ground black pepper

First, prepare the dressing. Lightly whisk all the ingredients together in a small bowl. Season to taste and set aside.

Now, to cook the peaches. Lightly grease a griddle pan or BBQ with the oil and then get it nice and hot. You may have to work in batches, depending on the size of your pan. Place the peach quarters, cut-side down, on the griddle pan or BBQ for 1–2 minutes to get the nice chargrilled marks. Use a metal fish slice to help lift the quarters up so as not to leave the chargrilled marks behind, then turn them onto their other cut side for another minute (don't cook on their skin side). The charring will add to the flavour. You can use a frying pan to char them, but obviously you won't get the chargrilled lines, though that is okay. Set the peaches cut-side up on a large serving platter as you go.

Arrange the mozzarella or burrata chunks around the peaches and scatter the rocket and basil leaves over. Scatter a little salt and pepper on top. Quickly whisk up the dressing again, if necessary, drizzle it over and serve.

CHARGRILLED CHICKEN, CARROT AND PEANUT SALAD WITH SWEET MANGO DRESSING

SERVES
6–8

When you are cooking the chilli flakes (along with the chicken) in this dish, please do be sure to open the windows and turn on the extractor fan, as that chilli sure does hit the back of the throat as it heats up!

4 x 150g skinless chicken breasts, cut into 2cm wide strips
Spray oil or 1 tbsp sunflower oil
½–1 tsp chilli flakes, depending how hot you like it (optional)
2 medium carrots
2 yellow peppers, deseeded
2 Golden Delicious apples
Leaves from ½ bunch of fresh mint
Leaves from ½ bunch of fresh coriander
50g roasted (not dry-roasted) peanuts, roughly chopped or crushed

SWEET MANGO DRESSING
1 small ripe mango, peeled and de-stoned and cut into really tiny cubes
6 tbsp extra virgin olive oil
2 tbsp white wine vinegar
Juice of ½ lime
Sea salt and freshly ground black pepper

Get a large griddle or frying pan nice and hot on a high heat. Depending on their size, you may need to use two, or alternatively cook the chicken in two batches. Toss the chicken strips in a large bowl with the oil, chilli flakes (if using) and salt and pepper. Lay the pieces in the hot pan(s) to cook for about 5–6 minutes, turning once, until cooked through. Once cooked, remove from the pan, pop them onto a plate and leave to cool.

Next, make the salad dressing by simply whisking all the ingredients together in a small bowl. Season to taste and set aside.

I like my carrots in ribbons rather than shreds for this recipe, so take a peeler and just keep peeling the carrots into ribbons until there's no carrot left, popping them onto a large serving platter as you go. Alternatively, you could use a mandolin or really sharp knife if you are confident in slicing them quite thin.

Next, slice the peppers into long, thin strips, adding them to the platter also. Then, quarter and core the apples before thinly slicing them into matchsticks. Add the apple slices to the salad and rip over the mint and coriander leaves. Add the cooled chicken and dressing and toss everything together gently. Sprinkle over the peanuts and serve.

CHARGRILLED GREEN BEAN, SUGAR SNAP AND COURGETTE SALAD WITH A POPPY SEED DRESSING

SERVES
4–6

For this recipe you need to use all of the frying pans you can. I tweeted recently to find out how many people owned and the responses showed that my average Twitter user had three frying pans – so do get them out! Also griddle pans are great for this recipe. Vegetables are naturally good for your health, but a chargrilled, roasted or pan-fried veggie is far nicer on the palate, adding a lot more flavour, and easier on the eye.

3 small to medium courgettes, trimmed
4 tsp sunflower or olive oil
300g fine beans, trimmed
200g sugar snaps or mangetout, sliced diagonally into 5mm wide strips
70g bag of rocket
1 red onion, halved and very finely sliced
½ bunch of fresh chives, very finely chopped (to give about 3 tbsp)
1 red chilli, deseeded for less heat if preferred, finely sliced (optional)

POPPY SEED DRESSING
2 tbsp extra virgin olive oil
1 tbsp balsamic vinegar
½ tsp poppy seeds
Sea salt and freshly ground black pepper

EQUIPMENT
Three large griddle or frying pans

Place three large griddle or frying pans (or a mixture of both) on a high heat on the hob. Alternatively, you can use fewer pans and take that little bit longer working in batches. Cut the courgettes into long, thin slices using a vegetable peeler, mandolin or sharp knife and gently toss the slices in a large bowl with 3 teaspoons of the oil until evenly coated. Carefully lay the slices down flat in a single layer in the hot pans and cook for about 1 minute on each side until charred and softened. Use tongs to remove them carefully onto a large serving platter.

Now toss all the green beans in the original bowl with the remaining teaspoon of oil until evenly coated. Pop them into the pans, again in a single layer, and cook for 3–4 minutes, tossing regularly, until they begin to go slightly brown, but still retain some crispness. Once cooked, tip onto the platter also. You are now finished with the pans, phew!

Scatter the rocket, onion and chives over the vegetables on the platter. Then quickly whisk the dressing ingredients together with salt and pepper or shake them in a jam jar secured with a tight-fitting lid. Drizzle the dressing over the salad and then get your (clean!) hands in and toss everything together really well. Garnish with strips of red chilli, if using, scattered on top and serve.

CHICKEN, FENNEL, WATERCRESS AND APPLE SALAD WITH PECORINO CHEESE

SERVES
6

I am always on the lookout for new salads as I am a bit of a salad monster and am constantly looking for new things for my lunch box. Pecorino cheese can be used interchangeably with Parmesan for this recipe. I think fennel is one of those ingredients that is a bit of an acquired taste for some, but the balance of the other flavours means it works really well in this dish.

1 tbsp sunflower oil
4 x 150g raw or cooked skinless chicken breasts
1 large fennel bulb, finely sliced, fronds reserved
75g bag of watercress
2 Granny Smith apples, quartered, cored and thinly sliced
25g pecorino or Parmesan cheese
Handful of pomegranate seeds (optional)

DRESSING
4 tbsp extra virgin olive oil
Finely grated zest and juice of 1 lemon
1 tsp caster sugar (optional)
Sea salt and freshly ground black pepper

If you are using raw chicken breasts, heat the oil in a large frying pan over a medium heat. Cut the chicken into short 1cm thick slices and then season them well. Fry the chicken in the pan for 5–6 minutes, stirring regularly, or until they are completely cooked through and the juices run clear. Then scatter them over a large serving platter and leave them to cool down a bit. If you are using ready-cooked chicken breasts, then just rip them into bite-sized pieces over the platter.

Whisk all the dressing ingredients together in a mug, using the sugar if you like a hint of sweetness, and season well with salt and pepper.

Once the chicken is cool, add the fennel, watercress and apple. Drizzle the dressing over and toss everything together well. Then, using a vegetable peeler, shave over the pecorino or Parmesan. Finish with a scattering of reserved fennel fronds and the pomegranate seeds, if using, and serve.

FOUR BEAN SALAD WITH MINT AND CHIVES AND A HONEY LIME DRESSING

SERVES
4–6

Vegetarians looking for a filling and tasty storecupboard salad, this one is for you – and best of all it's really quick and simple. I make this often and put a big batch of it in a Tupperware container in the fridge so that the family can dig in and help themselves when they are feeling a little peckish. Of course, this is a great one to take to the office for lunch.

410g tin of borlotti beans,
   drained and rinsed
410g tin of kidney beans,
   drained and rinsed
410g tin of cannellini beans,
   drained and rinsed
410g tin of haricot beans,
   drained and rinsed
1 bunch of spring onions,
   finely sliced
Handful of fresh chives, finely
   chopped (to give about 1 tbsp)

HONEY LIME DRESSING
2 tbsp extra virgin olive oil
Juice of 1 lime
Squidge of honey
Leaves from ½ bunch of fresh mint,
   finely chopped (to give
   about 2 tbsp)
Sea salt and freshly ground
   black pepper

Whisk all of the dressing ingredients in a large bowl and season to taste. Toss the beans, spring onion and chives through until well mixed and serve.

VIETNAMESE CHICKEN AND PEANUT SALAD WITH SESAME AND LIME

SERVES
4

When my daughter was eight (which seems a long time ago, she is well into her teens now!) I took her on a four-week trip to South East Asia. We visited Thailand, Cambodia, Laos and Vietnam and did cooking classes in each country. We made a salad similar to this, but used green papaya in it too, which is hard to get easily in the UK. I fell in love with the balance of flavours and that every mouthful gave you something else. If you have not tried Vietnamese food, I highly recommend it.

400ml tin of coconut milk
3 x 150g skinless, boneless chicken breasts, cut into big bite-sized slices
200g beansprouts
Juice of 2 limes
1 tbsp fish sauce
2 tsp sugar
1 red onion, thinly sliced
50g salted peanuts
3 tbsp sesame seeds
2 red chillies, deseeded for less heat if preferred, finely sliced
Leaves from 1 bunch of fresh mint (to give 4 tbsp)
Leaves from 1 bunch of fresh basil (to give 4 tbsp)
Leaves from 1 bunch of fresh coriander (to give 4 tbsp)
Sea salt and freshly ground black pepper

Bring the coconut milk to the boil in a medium pan over a medium heat. Add the chicken and a little salt and leave to simmer for 8 minutes before stirring in the beansprouts. Simmer for 2 more minutes or until the chicken is cooked through and the beansprouts wilted. Once ready, drain the chicken and beansprouts in a colander set over a bowl to catch the coconut milk and set everything aside to cool.

Place the lime juice and fish sauce in a large bowl and stir in the sugar until dissolved. Toss the red onion through and leave to sit for a few minutes until slightly softened. This also helps to take the rawness from the onion.

Meanwhile, bash the peanuts, sesame seeds and chillies together in a pestle and mortar and then tip this in with the red onion mixture. Add a couple of tablespoons of the drained coconut milk to loosen everything slightly. Add the mint, basil and coriander and then the reserved chicken and beansprouts and toss everything together well. Season to taste with salt and pepper and serve at once.

Top tip
The leftover coconut milk works wonderfully in a butternut squash soup, so either use it straight away or pop it in the freezer until needed.

LARB GAI – NICE AND SPICY THAI CHICKEN SALAD

SERVES
4

I know it's so simple to buy the chicken already minced up, but the problem with that stuff is you don't know what you're getting and it often has loads of fat and a bit of gristle in it, so it's always best to buy your own chicken and then mince it up yourself. I first had these in Thailand from a market stall, rammed full of chillies and a perfect balance of sweet, salty, sour and heat. I have tried to recreate that Asian flavour here. I hope you enjoy it!

2 large skinless, boneless chicken breasts (about 225g each)
1 tbsp sunflower oil
2 tbsp fish sauce
Juice of 1 lime
1 tsp caster, granulated or soft light brown sugar
3 spring onions, finely chopped
¼ cucumber, finely diced
1–2 red chillies, deseeded for less heat if preferred, finely sliced
1cm piece of fresh ginger, peeled and finely chopped
Leaves and stalks from ½ bunch of fresh coriander, roughly chopped (about 2 tbsp)
Leaves from ½ bunch of fresh mint, ripped
Handful of salted (but not dry roasted) peanuts (about 50g)
12 largish crisp iceberg lettuce leaves (cup shaped are best)
Flaked sea salt and freshly ground black pepper

Cut the chicken into large chunks and then blend in a food processor for around 10 seconds until chopped up quite small. Alternatively, very finely chop the chicken by hand.

Drizzle the oil into a large frying pan over a high heat. Add the minced chicken with salt and pepper and cook for 4–5 minutes, stirring regularly and breaking it up as you do so, until it turns from pink to white. Cut a piece open to check it is cooked and then tip the chicken into a colander set over a bowl. Leave to cool for 5 minutes so it won't cause the herbs to wilt, while also allowing any excess liquid to drain off, if necessary.

Pour the fish sauce and lime juice into a large bowl and stir in the sugar until dissolved. Add the spring onion, cucumber, chilli, ginger, coriander, all but a small handful of the mint leaves and the peanuts and stir together well. Tip the chicken in and toss it through. Taste it and check to see if it needs a little bit more of anything to get it just to your liking.

Arrange three lettuce leaves on each of four serving plates and place a couple of spoonfuls of the mixture into each one. Scatter the remaining mint leaves over to garnish and serve. The best way to eat these is to simply pick up a lettuce cup with your hands and tuck in.

KALE, HAZELNUT AND GRUYÈRE SALAD WITH A LIME AND BLACK PEPPER DRESSING

SERVES
4–6

Stateside they have baby kale, which is softer and sweeter and easier to prepare than standard kale. We don't seem to have it on sale over here yet, so if you know any kale farmers out there, please do give them a nudge! The prepared kale in the shops is fine, but just take a little time to remove the woody stems to make this dish easier to eat. This salad is very fresh and zingy and would go well with some grilled chicken on the top.

50g blanched hazelnuts
100g kale
50g young spinach leaves
1 bunch of fresh chives, cut into 1–2cm sticks
45g Gruyère cheese, cut into very, very small pieces

LIME AND BLACK PEPPER DRESSING
2 tbsp extra virgin olive oil
Juice of 1 lime
1 tsp maple syrup or honey
Sea salt and freshly ground black pepper

Toast the hazelnuts in a small pan (without oil in) on a medium heat for 4–5 minutes, tossing frequently, until golden. Tip onto a plate and leave to cool completely.

Tear off any tough woody stems from the kale and then slice the leaves into 1cm wide strips. Toss into a large bowl along with the spinach leaves and chives and set aside.

Whisk together the dressing ingredients and season to taste with salt and pepper. Pour this on top of the salad, add the cooled hazelnuts and the Gruyère and then toss everything gently together. Arrange on a serving platter or in a salad bowl and serve.

MOROCCAN-RIBBONED CARROT SALAD WITH CHICKPEAS, CUMIN AND PAPRIKA

SERVES
6–8

A totally delicious and moreish (if you'll pardon the pun) salad with flavour and texture to boot. A grilled piece of fish or chicken would finish this off nicely for an extra-healthy protein punch.

2 tbsp extra virgin olive oil
Juice of 1 lime
1 squidge of honey (optional)
2 tsp paprika
½ tsp ground cumin
Sea salt and freshly ground black pepper
3 big carrots
1 large red onion, very finely sliced
400g tin of chickpeas, drained
2 handfuls of raisins (about 50g) (optional)
Leaves from ½ bunch of fresh parsley or mint, roughly chopped or torn (to give 2 tbsp)
Generous handful of toasted flaked almonds (about 25g)

First, make the dressing. Put the oil, lime juice, honey (if using), paprika, cumin and a little salt and pepper into a small mug and whisk together with a fork. Set aside.

Thinly slice the carrots into wide ribbons using a vegetable peeler or mandolin. Toss them on a large serving plate with the red onion, chickpeas, raisins (if using) and all but a small handful of the parsley or mint.

Briefly mix the dressing again and pour it all over the salad, tossing everything together well to coat. Sprinkle with the remaining parsley or mint along with the toasted almonds and serve.

Top tip
To toast the almonds, place a medium-sized pan on a medium heat (without any oil). Tip in the almonds and gently toast, moving them around from time to time to prevent burning. Once they are lovely and golden, take off the heat and set aside to cool.

I DON'T KNOW THE KEY TO SUCCESS,
BUT THE KEY TO FAILURE IS TRYING
TO PLEASE EVERYBODY.

BILL COSBY

MAINS: CHICKEN

QUICK-COOK CHICKEN PICCATTA WITH SHALLOTS AND LEMON AND PARSLEY PASTA

SERVES
4

Chicken, chicken, chicken. I am always developing recipes to make chicken tasty and different. I love this dish for my family at the end of the day; it is super quick to cook and has a really good flavour to it. Tagliatelle is my pasta of choice, but spaghetti or linguine, or even my daughter's favourite conchiglie pasta, have featured in this dish when I have cooked it over the years, so please feel free to use your family's favourite.

4 x 150–200g skinless, boneless chicken breasts
1 tbsp olive oil
4 shallots, finely chopped
150ml white wine
150ml chicken stock
Juice of 1 small lemon
3 tbsp capers, drained
2 knobs of butter
Sea salt and freshly ground black pepper

PARSLEY PASTA
400g tagliatelle
Leaves from ½ bunch fresh flat-leaf parsley, roughly chopped
2 knobs of butter

Put a large pan of salted water on to boil for the pasta.

Lay two chicken breasts, spaced apart, between two pieces of cling film or parchment paper and then bash them out to about 1cm thick with a rolling pin or the bottom of a small pan. Repeat with the remaining two breasts and then season them all well.

Drizzle the oil in a large frying pan (or two if you think all four breasts won't fit) over a medium to high heat. Once hot, add the chicken breasts and cook for about 2 minutes on each side until golden brown.

Transfer the chicken breasts to a plate, cover with tin foil and set aside for the moment. Add the shallots to the frying pan (use just one pan now if you were using two) and cook on a medium heat for 4–5 minutes or until soft, but not coloured. Then turn the heat up to high and add the white wine and stock. Leave it to boil away for about 5 minutes until reduced by half.

Meanwhile, pop the pasta into the boiling water to cook according to the packet instructions until *al dente*.

Once the sauce has reduced, place the chicken breasts back into the frying pan and leave to warm through for 3–4 minutes, basting them occasionally and turning over halfway through. Add the lemon juice and capers and cook for 1 minute more before removing from the heat.

Once cooked, drain the pasta well. Return it to the pan, toss the parsley and butter through and then divide it among four serving plates. Arrange a chicken breast on top of each one. Finally, whisk the butter through the sauce until it melts, season to taste, spoon it over the chicken and serve at once.

CHICKEN BREAST DIANE WITH SWEET POTATO MASH AND NUTMEG

SERVES
4

4 x 150g skinless, boneless chicken breasts
2 tbsp sunflower oil
250g chestnut mushrooms, finely chopped
4 shallots, finely chopped
Leaves from a few sprigs of fresh thyme (to give about 1 tsp)
1 garlic clove, finely chopped
300ml port or Madeira
2 tbsp Dijon mustard
5 dollops of crème fraîche (about 100g)

SWEET POTATO MASH
2 x 350g packs of prepared sweet potato and butternut squash
Large knob of butter
Pinch of freshly grated nutmeg (optional)
Sea salt and freshly ground black pepper

This dish comes from America and is usually made with steak. Since chicken is what I seem to eat so much of and steak I save for a more special occasion, I wanted to include in this book lots of easy chicken dishes that are quick to prepare at the end of a busy day. Traditionally, steak Diane would be flambéd at the dining table for the waiting guests, but I have put an easy twist on this, meaning the alcohol can just be bubbled away in the pan so you don't have to start setting alcohol alight for dinner after a long train ride home!

Put a medium pan of salted water on to boil (enough to cook the sweet potato and butternut squash).

Meanwhile, put some cling film (or parchment paper) on the work surface and sit two chicken breasts in the middle, but spaced apart. Season well with salt and pepper and lay another sheet of cling film (or parchment paper) on top. Bash the chicken breasts with a rolling pin or the base of a small pan until they are about 1cm thick. Repeat with the remaining two breasts.

Heat 1 tablespoon of the oil in a large frying pan (you may need to use two frying pans to accommodate all four chicken breasts, in which case, just split the oil) over a medium to high heat. Once hot, carefully lower the chicken breasts in and cook for about 3 minutes on each side or until they are completely cooked through. Once cooked, transfer them to a plate and cover loosely with tin foil, reserving the pan for now.

Once the water has boiled, add the butternut squash and sweet potato mix and leave to cook away for 6–8 minutes or until they are soft.

Add the remaining tablespoon of oil to the pan and set over a medium heat. Add the mushrooms, shallots and thyme and cook for 2–3 minutes, stirring regularly, until wilted and softened. Then add the garlic and cook for 1 minute more. Turn the heat right up, add the port or Madeira and let it bubble away for 2–3 minutes to get rid of the strong alcohol taste. Add the mustard and crème fraîche and simmer away for another minute. Season to taste and then finally add the chicken breasts and any resting juices into the sauce and simmer for 1–2 minutes to heat through.

Drain the cooked vegetables well and return them to the pan. Add the butter, salt and pepper and some nutmeg, if you fancy it. Roughly mash and divide it among the serving plates. Arrange a chicken breast on top of each pile of mash. Drizzle the sauce over and serve.

ROAST SESAME, SOY AND HONEY CHICKEN

SERVES
4–6

1.8kg whole chicken
1–2 garlic cloves, depending on size, finely sliced
2 tsp sunflower or vegetable oil, plus extra for greasing
2½ tbsp sesame seeds
4 tbsp honey
1 tbsp dark soy sauce
1 tbsp mirin (most supermarkets now sell it)
1 red chilli, finely chopped
2.5cm piece of fresh ginger, peeled and finely chopped
Flaked sea salt and freshly ground black pepper

I really wanted to bring some roast chicken to the book, but make it something different. Most of us frequent the standard roast chicken with garlic, lemon and the other usual suspects, so bringing a bit of tasty Asia to our familiar Sunday dish seemed to me like a good option. This does go with crispy roast potatoes, but is equally nice with some rice, quinoa and stir-fried green veg, or with bits torn off and eaten tucked in some warm wraps, too.

Preheat the oven to 200°C, (fan 180°C), 400°F, Gas Mark 6. Lightly grease a large piece of tin foil with oil and place it oiled-side up in a roasting tin. If your foil is not wide enough to line the tin, then lay a second piece across in the opposite direction.

Sit the chicken upright in the centre of the foil, bring up the sides and tuck in towards the chicken to make a tray to hold the cooking juices without burning. Make about ten to twelve slits on the chicken breasts and legs and slide a slither of garlic into each one. Season well with salt and pepper and drizzle with the sunflower or vegetable oil. Place in the oven for about 1½ hours, basting regularly.

Meanwhile, mix together the sesame seeds, honey, soy, mirin, chilli and ginger and set aside.

After 1 hour, remove the chicken from the oven and spoon the honey and sesame mixture all over. Then return to the oven for the remaining half hour, again remembering to baste regularly, this time without knocking the sesame seeds off the top.

Once the chicken has had its full cooking time, remove it from the oven and test to check that it is cooked. Put a sharp knife into the thickest part of the bird in the thigh and press down – any juices that run out should be clear and not pink at all. If the juices are not running clear, then return to the oven, testing it again every 5 minutes or so, until fully cooked. Once ready, transfer the chicken to a carving board, cover with tin foil and leave to rest for 15 minutes. This will make the bird much more succulent and juicy and allow the temperature in the bird to even out.

Tip the basting juices from the tin foil in the roasting tray into a small saucepan and spoon off any fat that rises to the surface. Warm the juices over a low heat and stir in any juices from the resting chicken. Once rested, carve the chicken and serve each portion with a little of the honey gravy.

CHICKEN AND CASHEW NUT STIR-FRY WITH HOISIN SAUCE AND FIVE-SPICE RICE

SERVES
4

Learning how to cook or having good dishes in your repertoire does not always have to be about fancy stuff. The good old stir-fry, which was one of the first things I learnt to cook, has served me in good stead for years and got me out of many a what-to-have-for-dinner rut. The trick is all in the flavour and a nice hot pan. The addition of five-spice in the rice gives a nice twist to our plain white (or brown) staple! I have recently developed an addiction to quinoa and am loving the stuff; some would also argue that it's much better for you than rice due to its higher protein content. Give it a whirl!

2 tsp five-spice powder
250g brown, white long-grain or basmati rice or quinoa
125g cashew nuts
1 tbsp sunflower oil
2 large skinless, boneless chicken breasts (about 225g each), cut into bite-sized chunks
1 red pepper, trimmed, deseeded and cut into strips
1 yellow pepper, trimmed, deseeded and cut into strips
1 orange pepper, trimmed, deseeded and cut into strips
1 bunch of spring onions, trimmed and cut into 3cm pieces
2–3 red chillies, deseeded for less heat if preferred, cut into fine strips
3cm piece of fresh ginger, peeled and cut into thin matchsticks
2 garlic cloves, finely chopped
1 tsp cornflour
100ml chicken stock
3 tbsp hoisin sauce (I found mine in the supermarket; if they don't have it, then just use soy sauce instead)
Large handful of fresh basil leaves
Flaked sea salt and freshly ground black pepper

First, to cook the rice, put the five-spice in the bottom of a medium pan over a low heat. Cook for 3–4 minutes until you start to smell the aromas, and then add the rice or quinoa along with a little salt and cook it according to the packet instructions.

Meanwhile, put the cashew nuts into a large wok (without any oil) over a medium heat and toast for about 3–4 minutes (until you can smell them), giving them a shake from time to time until golden all over. Then tip them onto a plate and set them aside.

Heat the oil in the wok with the heat turned up to high. Season the chicken pieces with salt and pepper and stir-fry for 4–5 minutes, stirring occasionally, until golden. Add the peppers, spring onions, chillies and ginger, and cook for 2–3 minutes, keeping the pan moving so nothing burns. Add the garlic and cook for another minute.

Place the cornflour in a small bowl with 2 teaspoons cold water and mix to a smooth paste. Add to the stir-fry along with the stock and hoisin sauce and let the sauce bubble away for 1–2 minutes until it thickens slightly. Toss the toasted cashew nuts into the pan and check that the chicken is cooked through. Remove from the heat.

The rice or quinoa should be cooked by now, so drain, season to taste, if need be, and then return to the pan to keep warm, if necessary.

Spoon the rice or quinoa onto each serving plate. Spoon the stir-fry onto it and rip up the basil leaves to scatter over. Serve immediately.

CHARGRILLED CHICKEN BREASTS ON LINGUINE WITH A CHILLI AND GARLIC SALSA PUTTANESCA

SERVES
4

Simple, hearty (but not too heavy) family fare with lots of flavour. This dish is not so much a looker on the plate, but I just love the big flavours from these everyday ingredients.

400g linguine (preferably wholewheat)
4 good-sized skinless, boneless chicken breasts
Leaves from 3 sprigs of fresh thyme
Spray oil or 1 tbsp olive oil

CHILLI AND GARLIC SALSA PUTTANESCA
1 tbsp olive oil
2 garlic cloves, finely sliced
2 x 400g tins of chopped tomatoes
2 tbsp tomato purée
Few shakes of Worcestershire sauce (really deepens the flavour)
12 pitted green or black olives, roughly chopped
1 tbsp capers, drained
8 anchovies, drained
2 tsp chilli flakes
1 tsp sugar (optional)
Leaves from ¼ bunch of fresh flat or curly leaf parsley, finely chopped (to give about 2 tbsp)
Sea salt and freshly ground black pepper

Cook the pasta in a large pan of boiling, salted water according to packet instructions until *al dente*.

For the chicken, put some cling film (or parchment paper) on the work surface and sit two chicken breasts in the middle, but spaced apart. Season well with salt and pepper and sprinkle half of the thyme over. Lay another sheet of cling film (or parchment paper) on top and then bash the chicken breasts with a rolling pin or the base of a small pan until they are about 1cm thick. Repeat with the remaining two breasts. Set aside for now.

Next, cook the sauce. Heat the oil in a medium sauté pan on a low heat. Add the garlic and cook gently for 30 seconds, stirring, until just turning golden but not burning. Add the tomatoes, tomato purée and Worcestershire sauce, turn up the heat to high to bring to the boil, and then reduce to medium and let it bubble away for 6–8 minutes, stirring occasionally, until the sauce has reduced by about a quarter. It will spit out a bit and get a little messy, but the flavour will be well worth it! »

CHARGRILLED CHICKEN BREASTS ON LINGUINE WITH A CHILLI AND GARLIC SALSA PUTTANESCA

(continued)

Meanwhile, place a large griddle or frying pan on a high heat. Use two pans if you think the four flattened-out chicken breasts won't fit in one, otherwise you can cook them in two batches. Rub or spray the oil over each side of the chicken breasts and then fry them for about 2 minutes on each side or until they are nicely charred or browned and cooked right through.

Once the pasta is ready, drain well and pop it back in the pan with the lid on to keep warm.

Add the olives, capers, anchovies and chilli flakes to the sauce. Heat through for a couple of minutes and then season to taste with salt and pepper (the anchovies and olives will add saltiness, so season carefully). Add the sugar if the sauce is a bit tart as it will take the edge off the acidity. Finally, stir the parsley through and remove from the heat.

Divide the pasta among four plates and top with a chicken breast. Spoon the sauce over and serve at once.

WHOLE ROAST THAI GREEN CURRY CHICKEN

SERVES
4–6

5 tbsp Thai green curry paste
2 tsp Thai fish sauce
1 tsp soft light brown sugar
Finely grated zest and juice
    of 1 large lime
1.8kg whole chicken
1 tsp sunflower or vegetable oil
400ml tin of coconut milk
Large handful of fresh coriander
    leaves, roughly chopped
Flaked sea salt and freshly ground
    black pepper

How many times have I eaten Thai chicken curry? Too many to remember, but never a whole Thai chicken! I was sitting in my kitchen staring at the large bird that I had just taken out of the fridge, thinking how can I make this chicken something different? A rummage in the bottom of the fridge produced a pot of green curry paste and the rest, as they say, is history!

Mix together the green curry paste, fish sauce, sugar and lime zest and juice in a large, deep bowl. Using a sharp knife, carefully slash the chicken a few times through the thickest parts of the breast and legs. Pop the leftover lime halves into the chicken cavity. Holding the chicken over the bowl, slather the marinade all over the breasts and legs. Then place it, breast-side down, into the bowl, cover and leave to marinate in the fridge for at least 1 hour, but up to 6 preferably.

When ready to cook the chicken, preheat the oven to 200°C, (fan 180°C), 400°F, Gas Mark 6. Take the chicken out of the marinade and place it, breast-side up, in a roasting tin. Drizzle over any remaining marinade from the bowl, season with salt and pepper and cover tightly with tin foil. Roast in the oven for 1½ hours, basting every so often and removing the foil after an hour.

Once the chicken has had its time, remove it from the oven and test to see if it is cooked by inserting a small sharp knife into the thickest part of the bird. I do it around the groin area of the chicken and then press down a bit – the juices should run clear. If the juices are not running clear, then return to the oven, testing it again every 5 minutes or so, until fully cooked. Once cooked, remove the chicken from the tin onto a carving board, cover with tin foil and leave to rest for 15 minutes. This will make the bird much more succulent and juicy and allow the temperature in the bird to even out.

Place the roasting tin over a low heat and spoon off any fat that rises to the surface of the juices. Tilting the pan to pool the liquid will make this easier. Stir in the coconut milk, scraping any sticky bits from the bottom of the tin. Bring the mixture to a gentle simmer and allow to bubble away for 2–3 minutes until thickened slightly. Pour any juices from the resting chicken in, stir in the coriander and season to taste with salt and pepper. Then pour the sauce into a gravy boat.

Once rested, serve the chicken with the sauce. You can accompany it with traditional roasties or some plain rice along with a simple salad or stir-fried vegetables, if preferred.

CREAMY CHICKEN KORMA WITH FRAGRANT RICE AND PEAS

SERVES
4

It's not the easiest thing in the world to replicate a chicken korma eaten in an Indian restaurant with a nice glass of something cool to drink. However, in the interests of home cooking, I have tried to make a dish with a little hint of India to eat at home.

6 cardamom pods
3 cloves
1 tbsp ground coriander
1 tbsp ground cumin
1 tsp ground cinnamon
1 tsp turmeric powder
1 tbsp sunflower oil
1 large onion, roughly diced
5cm piece of fresh ginger, peeled and very finely chopped
1–2 red chillies, deseeded for less heat if preferred, very finely chopped
4 x 150g skinless, boneless chicken breasts, cut into large bite-sized chunks
2 garlic cloves, very finely chopped
100g cashew nuts (not salted or roasted)
200g natural yogurt (preferably full-fat so that it does not curdle, but low-fat is fine)
200ml single cream
Coriander leaves, to serve (optional)
Sea salt and freshly ground black pepper

FRAGRANT RICE AND PEAS
250g quick-cook basmati rice
1 tsp turmeric or curry powder
100g frozen peas

Bash the cardamom pods open with a pestle and mortar or on a chopping board with a rolling pin or heavy-based pan and pop the seeds out into a large sauté or frying pan. Add the cloves, ground coriander, cumin, cinnamon and turmeric and cook over a low to medium heat for a few minutes until the spices begin to release their aromas.

Next, stir in the oil, onion, ginger and chilli and cook for about 5 minutes, or until the onion is just beginning to soften.

Meanwhile, put the rice on to cook according to pack instructions. Add the turmeric or curry powder to the salted, boiling water at the start of cooking. Add the peas halfway through.

Season the chicken well with salt and pepper and then, once the onion mixture is ready, tip the chicken breasts into the pan and turn up the heat. Cook for 2–3 minutes until the chicken is sealed all over, stirring regularly. Add the garlic and the cashew nuts and cook for 1 more minute. Add the yogurt and cream, pop the lid on and leave to simmer away for 8–10 minutes or until the chicken is cooked through (with no pink flesh in the middle).

Once your rice is ready, drain it if necessary, then set aside in the pan with the lid on to keep warm.

Season the sauce to taste and then divide the rice among four serving plates with the korma sauce on top. Finish with some coriander leaves, if you fancy it.

CHICKEN SAUTERNES WITH MUSHROOM, TARRAGON AND PEA, LEMON AND BLACK PEPPER RICE

SERVES
4

If you can, get your hands on a good bottle of Sauternes – though a bit expensive it really is worth it. It adds a real depth of flavour that you can't get with a regular white wine. Either way, if you can use a good chicken stock, then you will still get good flavour into this fresh chicken dish.

1 tbsp sunflower oil
8 skinless, boneless chicken thighs
1 large onion, thickly sliced
2 garlic cloves, finely chopped
Large knob of butter
2 tbsp plain flour
250ml Sauternes or white wine
300ml good-quality chicken stock
250g chestnut mushrooms, finely sliced
Leaves from ½ bunch of fresh tarragon, roughly chopped (to give about 2 tbsp)
3–4 dollops (about 75–100g) crème fraîche (optional)
Juice of 1 lemon

PEA, LEMON AND BLACK PEPPER RICE
250g long-grain or basmati rice (brown or white) or quinoa
Couple of handfuls of frozen peas (about 100g)
Finely grated zest of 1 lemon
Sea salt and freshly ground black pepper

Place a large sauté or frying pan on a high heat with the oil in it. Season the chicken thighs really well and then brown them off for about 3 minutes per side to get some good colour on them (but they will not yet be cooked through). Then, remove them from the pan onto a plate and set aside.

Next, reduce the heat to medium, add the onion to the pan and brown them for 2–3 minutes, stirring often. Add the garlic, butter and flour, stirring well until it becomes almost paste-like, and cook for a moment. Return the heat to high and pour in the wine gradually, while stirring. Scrape any sticky chicken bits from the bottom of the pan as you go. While continuing to stir, allow it to bubble away for 2–3 minutes until thickened.

Next, gradually stir in the stock until well blended. Add the mushrooms and nestle the chicken pieces, skin-side up, into the sauce. Add any resting juices from the chicken in too. Sprinkle the tarragon over, bring to the boil and then reduce to simmer away gently for 20 minutes.

As this simmers away, cook the rice or quinoa in a large pan of salted water according to pack instructions. Five minutes before it is ready, throw in the frozen peas, lemon zest, some salt and a good amount of freshly ground black pepper. Drain the rice or quinoa if necessary, return to the pan and pop a lid on to keep warm.

After 20 minutes, the sauce will have reduced a little and the chicken should be completely cooked through. Remove the chicken from the sauce onto a plate and keep warm. Stir the crème fraîche, if using, and lemon juice into the sauce and warm through for a minute or two. Check the seasoning, adjusting if necessary.

Spoon the rice or quinoa onto each serving plate. Sit two chicken pieces on top, spoon the sauce over and serve at once.

MOROCCAN-FLAVOURED ROAST LEMON CHICKEN WITH CUMIN ROAST NEW POTATOES AND MINTED PEAS

SERVES
4–6

I went to my local supermarket to buy chicken and all the trimmings for the family Sunday lunch, brought it back home and then thought we all, Chez LP, needed a bit of a change. So I rifled through the spice rack, put together a huddle of North African spices and set about sending this Big British Roast right the way down the spice route. The list of ingredients is not the shortest, but quite a lot are ones that are usually knocking about most kitchens, and the others are very easy to get. I find it is good to have a few different chicken roasts under your Sunday cheffing belt!

MARINADE
2 tsp ground cinnamon
2 tsp ground cumin
2 tsp ground coriander
2 tsp paprika
2 tsp turmeric powder
4 tbsp sunflower oil
2 garlic cloves, crushed
Squidge of honey
Juice of ¼ lemon (about 1 tsp)
4 sprigs of fresh thyme, finely chopped (to give about 1 tsp)

ROAST LEMON CHICKEN
1.8kg whole chicken
2 garlic cloves
1 large onion, cut into eighths
1 lemon, cut in half

CUMIN ROAST NEW POTATOES
1kg new potatoes
1 tbsp sunflower oil or spray oil
2 tbsp cumin seeds

KICK-ARSE GRAVY
200ml red or white wine (or just replace this with an extra 200ml of the chicken stock)
1 tbsp plain flour
250ml good-quality chicken stock
½ tsp Marmite
Few shakes of Worcestershire sauce
Knob of butter (optional)

MINTED PEAS
600g fresh or frozen peas
Leaves from 1 bunch of fresh mint or coriander, to finish
Sea salt and freshly ground black pepper

Mix all of the marinade ingredients together in a large bowl with 2 tablespoons water. Then, using a sharp knife, carefully slash the chicken a few times through the thickest parts of the breast and legs. Holding the chicken over the bowl, slather the marinade all over the breasts and legs. Then place it breast-side down into the bowl, cover and leave to marinate in the fridge for at least 1 hour, but up to 6 preferably.

When ready to cook the chicken, preheat the oven to 200°C, (fan 180°C), 400°F, Gas Mark 6. Slam the garlic cloves with the side of a large knife or base of a pan and toss into a roasting tray with the onion wedges. Take the chicken out of the marinade and place it breast-side up in the roasting tin. Smear any marinade remaining in the bowl over the chicken and season with salt and pepper. The chicken doesn't look pretty at this point, but don't worry, it will be amazing once roasted! Pop the lemon halves into the chicken cavity and roast in the oven for 1½ hours, basting every so often. Cover loosely with tin foil after 45 minutes.

About half an hour before the chicken is ready, prepare the potatoes for the oven. Toss them in a roasting tray with the oil and then scatter over the cumin seeds and some salt and pepper. Toss everything together and pop in the oven to roast for 40–50 minutes. ≫

MOROCCAN-FLAVOURED ROAST LEMON CHICKEN WITH CUMIN ROAST NEW POTATOES AND MINTED PEAS

(continued)

Once the chicken has had its time, remove it from the oven and test to see if it is cooked by inserting a small, sharp knife into the thickest part of the bird. I do it around the groin area of the chicken and then press down a bit – the juices should run clear. If the juices are not running clear, then return to the oven, testing it again every 5 minutes or so until fully cooked. Once cooked, tip the chicken up to allow the juices to run out of the cavity into the tray. Then, transfer the chicken onto a plate and leave covered in the foil to rest for 15 minutes. This will allow the chicken to become more juicy and the temperature in the bird to even out.

Put the roasting tin on a medium to high heat. If your roasting tin will not go on the hob, then just tip the cooking juices into a medium pan. Leave all of the garlic and onion in the mix, as this will make some seriously delicious gravy. Once the juices are bubbling, add the wine and bubble it down for 2–3 minutes. Meanwhile, blend the flour and 2 tablespoons of water to a smooth paste. Stir this into the reduced wine mixture and bubble away for about 1 minute, stirring constantly to avoid any lumps forming. Next, stir in the stock, Marmite and Worcestershire sauce, turn the heat right up and allow to boil away for 8–10 minutes, stirring regularly, until reduced and thickened.

Meanwhile, put the peas on to cook according to packet instructions.

Check the potatoes are tender through when pierced with a knife and then remove from the oven.

To finish the gravy, pour it through a sieve over a large jug and, using the back of a spoon, squish the onion garlic mix through the sieve as much as you can. Really get in there and get all those lovely flavours out from the veg. Once you have squidged the mix almost dry, scrape the underside of the sieve and add that into the gravy too, discarding anything remaining inside the sieve. Put the gravy back into the roasting tin/pan and just heat it back through. Season to taste and pour into a warmed gravy jug.

Once cooked, drain the peas, return them to the pan and season with salt and pepper.

Divide the potatoes among the plates, slice up the rested chicken and place on top of the tatties with the peas to the side and then pour over the gravy. Then rip over mint or coriander leaves and serve.

Top tip
For an extra silky and rich sauce, add a knob of butter (a bit naughty, but by gosh it is nice).

CREOLE CHICKEN AND PRAWN JAMBALAYA

SERVES
4–6

This dish has some spice, so do lessen the heat a little if you have a non-spice eating guest!

3 tsp sunflower oil
3 skinless, boneless chicken thighs, cut into bite-sized pieces
4 full-flavoured sausages, such as venison or sweet chilli pork, cut into 2cm slices
2 large onions, finely sliced
1 tsp fennel seeds
3 garlic cloves, finely chopped
1 tbsp smoked paprika
2 tsp cayenne pepper
Leaves from 2 sprigs of fresh thyme (to give about 2 tsp)
1 bay leaf
200ml white wine (or just use 800ml of stock in total)

600ml good-quality chicken stock
400g tin of tomatoes
1 tbsp tomato purée
250g long-grain or basmati rice or quinoa
350g raw, shelled prawns (2 x 250g bags of frozen prawns should give about this weight once defrosted)
Leaves from ½ a bunch of fresh parsley, finely chopped, to serve
1 lemon, cut into wedges, to serve (optional)
Sea salt and freshly ground black pepper

Get 2 teaspoons of the oil nice and hot in a large pan on a medium to high heat. Season the chicken with salt and pepper and add it to the pan with the sausages. Brown the meat all over for 3–4 minutes, stirring regularly. Using a slotted spoon, scoop the meat out into a bowl, leaving the oil behind in the pan, and set aside.

Add the remaining teaspoon of oil to the pan, reduce the heat to medium and cook the onion for 4–5 minutes, stirring regularly, until just catching colour.

Meanwhile, grind the fennel seeds in a pestle and mortar until quite powdery. Add this to the onion along with the garlic, paprika, cayenne, thyme and bay leaf and cook for a minute more. Turn up the heat, add the white wine and allow it to bubble down for a minute, while scraping any sticky meat bits from the bottom of the pan. Add the stock, tomatoes and tomato purée and bring the mixture to the boil.

Reduce the heat, stir in the rice or quinoa, pop a lid on and leave it to cook for 20–25 minutes, stirring regularly to prevent it from sticking on the bottom.

Five minutes before the rice or quinoa is ready, tip in the chicken, sausages and prawns. Cook until everything is cooked through and the rice or quinoa is tender. Season to taste with salt and pepper and then serve sprinkled with parsley and with lemon wedges for squeezing, if you like.

WHOLE ROAST TANDOORI CHICKEN

SERVES
4–6

This chicken would be lovely served with roast potatoes, rice or griddled flatbreads, salad and minted yogurt. Just a quick note on the red food colouring – the supermarket ones are no longer very strong, but sugarpaste colours, which are specialist cake-making colours, are much better.

100g full-fat natural yogurt
2 tbsp fresh lemon juice
1 tsp ground coriander
1 tsp garam marsala (find it with the other spices in the supermarket)
1 tsp ground cumin
1 tsp medium or hot chilli powder
2.5cm piece of fresh ginger, peeled and finely grated
2 garlic cloves, crushed
¼–½ tsp red food colouring (optional) (see intro)
1.8kg whole chicken
Flaked sea salt and freshly ground black pepper

Mix the yogurt, lemon juice, spices, ginger, garlic and food colouring, if using, in a large, deep bowl. Using a sharp knife, carefully slash the chicken a few times through the thickest parts of the breast and legs. Holding the chicken over the bowl, slather the marinade all over the breasts and legs. Then place it, breast-side down, into the bowl, cover and leave to marinate in the fridge for at least 1 hour, but up to 6 preferably.

When ready to cook the chicken, preheat the oven to 200°C, (fan 180°C), 400°F, Gas Mark 6. Take the chicken out of the marinade and place it, breast-side up, in a roasting tin. Smear any marinade remaining in the bowl over the chicken, season with salt and pepper and cover loosely with tin foil. The chicken doesn't look pretty at this point, but don't worry, it will be amazing once roasted! Roast in the oven for 1½ hours, basting every so often and removing the foil after an hour.

Once the chicken has had its time, remove it from the oven and test to see if it is cooked by inserting a small sharp knife in to the thickest part of the bird. I do it around the groin area of the chicken and then press down a bit – the juices should run clear. If the juices are not running clear, then return to the oven, testing it again every 5 minutes or so, until fully cooked. Once cooked, cover with tin foil and leave to rest for 15 minutes. This will allow the chicken to become more juicy and the temperature in the bird to even out.

Once it has rested, remove the tin foil and serve with roast potatoes, rice or griddled flatbreads, salad and minted yogurt.

THE MOUTH SHOULD HAVE THREE GATE KEEPERS.
IS IT TRUE? IS IT KIND? AND IS IT NECESSARY?

ARAB PROVERB

MAINS:
PORK, BEEF
& LAMB

PORK LOIN RIBS WITH A SWEET AND SOUR GLAZE

SERVES
4

I included some ribs in my second book, *Home Cooking Made Easy*, which went down rather nicely at my family table. These are a little different, with a sweet-and-sour glaze, and even quicker and easier to make. I have suggested cutting the pork loin ribs up into smaller pieces, but if you can keep them as whole as possible, the ribs will remain more succulent. For me, these are lovely, lovely finger food.

PORK LOIN RIBS
2 tsp sunflower oil
2 x 600g rack of pork loin ribs, each cut into 4 portions
2 tbsp five-spice powder

SWEET AND SOUR GLAZE
6 tbsp ketchup
6 tbsp balsamic vinegar or rice vinegar
4 tbsp dark soy sauce
4 squidges of honey

4cm piece of fresh ginger, peeled and very finely diced
2 red chillies, deseeded for less heat if preferred, very finely chopped
Flaked sea salt and freshly ground black pepper

GARNISH
1 spring onion

Preheat the oven to 200°C, (fan 180°C), 400°F, Gas Mark 6.

Line a large roasting tray with tin foil and grease with the oil. Place the pork ribs in the roasting tin and rub the five-spice all over each side of them. Then roast in the oven for 2 hours (setting a timer for 30 minutes first of all).

Meanwhile, prepare the garnish. Trim and cut the spring onion in half across and then cut each piece into really thin lengthways strips. Pop them into a small bowl of iced water, cover and sit in the freezer until ready to serve.

Put all of the glaze ingredients together in a small pan, bring to the boil and then turn off the heat.

Once the ribs have been cooking for 30 minutes, remove from the oven. Using just half of the glaze for now, brush it over each side of the ribs. Cover them with tin foil and return to the oven for the remaining 1 hour 30 minutes. Reserve the remaining glaze in the pan for later.

A few minutes before the ribs are ready, reheat the remaining glaze. Arrange the cooked ribs on a large serving platter and pour the warm glaze evenly over. Drain the spring onion garnish from the iced water. They should now have curled nicely. Scatter them over the ribs to garnish and serve at once.

LAMB BARBACOA

SERVES
6–8

150ml apple, sherry
   or balsamic vinegar
6 garlic cloves, thinly sliced
1 red chilli, deseeded for less heat
   if preferred, finely sliced
Leaves from ½ bunch of fresh
   thyme (to give 2 tbsp)
2 tsp dried oregano
2 tsp ground cinnamon
2 tsp ground cumin
½–1 tsp chilli flakes, depending
   how hot you like it
1 tsp ground allspice

2 whole cloves
2kg lamb shoulder on the bone or
   2.5kg leg of lamb on the bone
1 tbsp cornflour, to thicken
   (optional)
Sea salt and freshly ground
   black pepper

EQUIPMENT
Large slow cooker (optional)

This recipe was tested with both a lamb shoulder and the leg. The leg was my favourite as it had a lot more meat and less fat, but nevertheless I have given you the option here for both, as a shoulder is cheaper. The lamb joint is quite an awkwardly shaped one, and may not fit into your slow cooker or casserole dish, so do get the butcher to crack the bone so that it can fit.

Preheat the oven to 150°C, (fan 130°C), 300°F, Gas Mark 2. Check that the shelves are okay to fit the casserole dish in with the lid on, adjusting them if necessary.

Pour the vinegar into a large casserole dish and stir in the remaining ingredients (except the lamb and cornflour) until well blended. Add salt and pepper and then place the lamb shoulder or leg carefully inside. If you don't have a casserole dish, then use a deep-sided roasting tray and cover it tightly with a double layer of tin foil. Slow cook for about 3½ hours or until the meat is meltingly tender enough to cut with a spoon.

Once cooked, carefully lift the lamb out of the liquid onto a platter and cover with foil to keep warm. Bring the liquid to the boil on a high heat. Leave to bubble away for 15–20 minutes until it has reduced by a third. If you would prefer it to be thicker than it is, then blend the cornflour in a mug with 3 tablespoons of the lamb juices to form a paste. Whisk this into the pan and then turn up the heat to let everything boil away for 1–2 minutes until thickened.

Check the seasoning and serve the lamb juices with the sliced meat. This is great served with warmed wraps along with a bit of salad or just simply over some rice or with some roasted squash or cabbage.

Top tip
If using a slow cooker: Pour the vinegar into the slow cooker and stir in the remaining ingredients (except the lamb and cornflour) until well blended. Add salt and pepper and then place the lamb shoulder or leg carefully inside. Pop the lid on and set to low, then leave to slow cook for 6–8 hours until the lamb is meltingly tender. You should be able to cut it with a spoon. Once cooked, carefully lift the lamb out of the liquid onto a platter and reduce the sauce and serve as above.

SPICY CHILLI CON CARNE WITH PUMPKIN AND RED WINE

I usually overdo the chilli in this one as I love chilli so much, but please just add enough to make it just right for you so you don't blast your family's head off as I do sometimes! I have used pumpkin in this recipe, but sweet potato or a mix of both works just fine too. This is so tasty served with rice or stuffed in a potato, or with tortilla chips and dips, also.

1 tbsp sunflower oil
1 large onion, very finely chopped
2 garlic cloves, very finely chopped
500g lean minced beef
2 tsp ground cumin
1–3 tsp chilli powder, depending on how hot you want it!
Leaves from 2 stalks of fresh rosemary, very finely chopped (to give about 1 tbsp)
2 bay leaves
Small squidge of honey
1 large glass of red wine, Marsala or beef stock (about 200ml)

2 x 400g tins of chopped tomatoes
2 tbsp tomato purée
500g pumpkin (or butternut squash), peeled, deseeded and cut into large bite-sized cubes
Flaked sea salt and freshly ground black pepper

TO SERVE
Cooked white or brown rice
Handful of fresh coriander leaves
Lime wedges
Sour cream (optional)

Put the oil in a large pan on a medium heat. Add the onion and cook for 8 minutes until it begins to soften, stirring regularly. Then add the garlic and cook for 1 more minute.

Turn the heat up to high and add the minced beef, cumin, chilli powder, rosemary, bay leaves and honey and cook until the beef turns from pink to brown (about 2–3 minutes), stirring regularly. Add the red wine, Marsala or beef stock, tomatoes and tomato purée and bring it to the boil. Then, turn down the heat and leave it to simmer for 10 minutes, stirring occasionally.

Add the pumpkin pieces and cook for a further 20 minutes, stirring it from time to time so that nothing sticks to the bottom of the pan. The sauce should be reduced and thickened and the pumpkin tender when pierced with a knife.

Season the chilli well and then serve on a bed of steaming hot rice. Garnish with fresh coriander and serve with lime wedges and sour cream, if you like.

LOW AND SLOW BRAISED LAMB WITH SHERRY AND SOY

SERVES
6–8

This needs to go in a casserole dish with a lid, so make sure you have a pot big enough for it to go in. If you don't have one, which I don't, buy two half legs of lamb. Or if you want to leave the leg whole and don't have a casserole dish big enough, then use a deep-sided roasting tray and cover it tightly with a double layer of tin foil. Shoulder is cheaper with a lovely sweet meat; just get your butcher to crack the bone so that the lamb will fit into your dish.

2kg shoulder of lamb on the bone or 2.5kg leg of lamb on the bone
400g cherry tomatoes
5 garlic cloves, peeled and squashed
Leaves from 4 sprigs of fresh thyme (to give about 1 tbsp)
500ml good-quality beef stock
150ml dry sherry
100ml soy sauce
3 squidges of honey
3 carrots, cut into 2cm wide slices
2 leeks, cut into 2cm wide slices and washed well
Sea salt and freshly ground black pepper

Preheat the oven to 150°C, (fan 130°C), 300°F, Gas Mark 2. Check that the shelves are okay to fit the casserole dish in with the lid on, adjusting them if necessary.

Put the lamb in a large casserole dish and season it well. Scatter over the tomatoes, garlic and thyme. Mix the beef stock, sherry, soy sauce and honey together in a large jug and pour over the lamb. The vegetables go in at a later stage. Pop the lid on and place in the oven for 2 hours (it will need 3½ hours in total).

After this time, carefully remove the dish from the oven and add the carrot and the leek, using a spoon to push them down into the liquid. I add these vegetables at this point as they can disintegrate into a mush if they go in at the beginning of the cooking time. Return to the oven for another 1½ hours or until the lamb meat is literally just so soft that it falls off the bone. This usually takes 3½ hours, but can sometimes take up to 4.

Once the meat is ready, carefully lift it out from the dish onto a plate and cover with tin foil to keep warm. Bring the liquid in the casserole dish to the boil on a high heat (or if using a roasting tray, then pour the liquid into a wide pan). Leave it to boil away for 5–10 minutes, when the sauce will become a little thicker and even more flavourful. Finally check the seasoning, adjusting to taste if necessary. Carve the lamb and serve at once with the sauce.

SLOW AND LOW ROAST PORK BELLY WITH A SAGE, APRICOT AND FENNEL STUFFING AND KICK-ARSE CRACKLING

SERVES
4–6

1 tbsp fennel seeds
2 tsp coriander seeds
2 large garlic cloves, roughly chopped
8 sage leaves
Leaves from 6 sprigs of fresh thyme (to give about 1 tsp)
1 tbsp olive oil

1 tsp sea salt
½ tsp freshly ground black pepper
1.5kg boneless pork belly, skin scored
Handful of dried apricots (about 50g), roughly chopped
Sea salt and freshly ground black pepper

I wrote a recipe for slow-roast shoulder of pork in my second book *Home Cooking Made Easy* and people contacted me saying how much they loved cooking a roast pork. For some it was their first foray into the world of a low and slow roast pig. Pork belly for me is the first roast pork that I ate, and I remember the crunch of the crackling and then the softness of the meat and I also remember falling in love instantly. I have paired this recipe with pork's familiar friends: sage, apricot and fennel. All that it needs to go with it are some very crispy roast potatoes, some freshly minted peas and a good rich gravy.

Preheat the oven to 240°C, (fan 220°C), 475°F, Gas Mark 9.

Put the fennel and coriander seeds into a frying pan with no oil in it and cook on a medium heat for about 5 minutes until you start to smell the spices. Tip them into a pestle and mortar and add the garlic, sage, thyme, oil and salt and pepper, then bash the mixture to a paste.

Lay the pork belly, skin-side down, on a clean board and spread the paste all over, leaving a 2cm margin around the sides (if you put it right to the edges it just tends to squish out when you roll it). Scatter over the apricot pieces and then place the pork belly with one of the long sides facing you. From this edge, roll it away from you to make a tight sausage roll. Then use kitchen string to tie it at regular intervals to secure. There are elegant butcher ways of doing this tying up thing, and there are ways that just get the job done, and getting the job done is fine. It does help if there is another pair of hands to help you as you roll it up, but it can be done with one pair of hands – it's just a little bit more messy! »

Sit a wire rack over or in a roasting tin and then put the pork on top of that, seam-side down. Season the pork with some more salt and pepper and place into the oven to cook for 20 minutes (it will need another 3 hours). I put the extractor fan on at this point as the smoke that comes from the oven is immense!

After the 20 minutes, which I like to call 'the crackling stint', turn the oven temperature down to 150°C, (fan 130°C), 300°F, Gas Mark 2 and just leave the joint to cook for another 3 hours.

Remove the pork from the oven and leave to rest for 10–15 minutes. Snip and remove the string and, using a sharp knife, carefully cut into thick slices and serve.

Top tip
If you can't find a wire rack that will fit in the oven, that is okay. Cooking it wire-rack-style just means that air can circulate around the meat as it cooks so it will cook more evenly, but it is fine if you don't have one.

SLOW-AND-STEADY BOLOGNESE SAUCE WITH ROSEMARY AND GARLIC

SERVES
4–6

If your family are anything like mine, wholewheat spaghetti receives an emphatic no at my house. So, I had to take matters into my own hands in a bid to get them to eat it. Each time we had spaghetti, or any other of its Italian friends, I would substitute the tiniest portion of its better-received white cousin for a little of the wholewheat hearty stuff. We are now at 80 per cent wholewheat pasta and 20 per cent of the other stuff and so far not a peep of a complaint from the hungry mouths at the kitchen table. Give it a go, little by little. week by week; smother it with a good sauce and hopefully they will never know. It can be our little secret!

2 tsp sunflower oil
1kg lean minced beef
2 rashers of Danish smoked back bacon, trimmed of any fat, finely diced
2 x 400g tins of chopped tomatoes
200ml red wine or beef stock
1 large onion, very finely chopped
1 carrot, finely chopped
1 stick of celery, finely chopped
2 garlic cloves, finely chopped
2 tbsp tomato purée
Leaves from 1 sprig of fresh rosemary, finely chopped (to give about 1 tsp)
1 tbsp dried oregano
1 bay leaf
400g spaghetti, preferably wholewheat
1 tsp sugar (optional)
Leaves from ½ bunch of fresh basil or flat-leaf parsley, roughly chopped
Sea salt and freshly ground black pepper

EQUIPMENT
Slow cooker (optional)

Heat the oil in a large frying pan over a high heat. Working in batches, sear the minced beef for about 4–5 minutes, stirring occasionally, until brown all over. Use a slotted spoon to scoop it out into the slow cooker bowl as you go, leaving the oil behind in the pan for the next batch. Sear the bacon in the same way. I did think I could skip this step, but the meat tasted rather unpleasant, so browning the meat seems to be a crucial step in getting a tasty spag bol.

Add all the remaining ingredients, except the pasta, sugar and basil or parsley to the slow cooker. Stir well together and season with salt and pepper. Pop on the lid and cook for 6–7 hours on low.

About 10 minutes (or however long it says on the spaghetti packet) before the sauce is ready, cook the pasta according to the pack instructions. Once ready, drain and set aside with a lid on to keep warm.

Taste the bolognese sauce and adjust the seasoning to just the way you like it. If the sauce is too tart, add the sugar to sweeten it slightly.

Tip the pasta into the sauce, add the basil or parsley and stir through, then divide among four or six bowls and serve.

Top tip
Conventional hob method: Sear the meat as above, then remove from the pan using a slotted spoon. Fry the onion, carrot, celery, rosemary, oregano and bay leaf over a low heat for 8–10 minutes until softened. Add the garlic for 1 final minute. Then add the meat back in, turn up the heat and add the wine. Allow everything to bubble down for a few minutes (if using just beef stock there's no need to do this). Add the chopped tomatoes, tomato purée and the sugar. Cover with a lid and simmer on a gentle heat for 1–1½ hours until rich and thickened.

CHINESE CHAR SIU-STYLE PORK

SERVES
8–10

150g hoisin sauce
75ml soy sauce
4 tsp sesame oil
2 tsp five-spice powder
5 garlic cloves, finely chopped
5cm piece of fresh ginger,
  peeled and finely grated
3kg boneless pork shoulder,
  rind removed
250ml cold vegetable
  or chicken stock

TO SERVE
Rice, to serve (optional)
Freshly ground black pepper

EQUIPMENT
Slow cooker

I have named this char siu-style pork as I am aware that traditionally this pork is barbecued and usually contains other exotic ingredients, such as rice wine and bean curd. However, in the name of keeping things simple and not having to search the internet endlessly for a Chinese supermarket within your reach, I have written the recipe in char siu-style, offering a gentle nod to the Cantonese classic. You will need a large slow cooker to make this in, and the char siu-style pork is particularly delicious served with some Asian greens if you fancy it.

If, and only if, you have time, marinate the pork first of all. Mix the hoisin sauce, soy sauce, sesame oil, five-spice, garlic and ginger together in a large bowl, baking dish or food storage bag. Add the pork in, tossing and massaging to coat. Cover and store in the fridge for a few hours or overnight. If you are like the large majority of us, not blessed with oodles of time or patience to marinate and then slow cook, then just begin with the slow-cook stage.

Put the marinade ingredients into the slow cooker with a good amount of pepper. Toss the pork in the marinade if you haven't already done so earlier and then pour the stock over. Pop the slow cooker lid on and cook on the low setting for 7–8 hours until cooked through and very tender.

After this time, remove the pork from the slow cooker onto a plate to keep warm and then pour the juices into a large, wide pan over a high heat. Let the mixture bubble away for 10–15 minutes or so until it reduces and thickens a little.

Whilst this is happening, now is a good time to cook some rice, if you fancy your pork with it. Once the sauce is thickened, season to taste if necessary and serve with pork slices and the rice. Delish.

LAMB ROGAN JOSH WITH SAFFRON BASMATI RICE

SERVES
4

I know it is all too easy to order in a curry or, for that matter, get one of the many ready meals from the shops, but for me there is often beauty to be found in making a Rogan Josh from scratch. Traditionalists will know that it is usually made with ghee, butter that has been heated and then had the milk solids skimmed off, but in praise of keeping things simple, I am using sunflower oil for this recipe. Paprika gives the heat in this, but if you want to turn things up a notch, do feel free to throw in some red-hot chilli peppers, if you fancy blasting your co-eaters socks off.

1–2 tbsp sunflower oil
750g lamb leg steaks, fat and bone removed and meat cut into large chunks
1 large onion, sliced into thick chunks
2 bay leaves
3 cardamom pods, slammed open
3 cloves
1 tbsp ground cinnamon
1 tbsp ground coriander
1 tbsp ground cumin
1 tbsp paprika
1 tsp garam masala
200ml natural or Greek yogurt, full- or low-fat
4cm piece of fresh ginger, peeled and roughly chopped
5 garlic cloves (a lot, I know, but worth it), roughly chopped
400g tin of chopped tomatoes
1 tbsp tomato purée
Handful of fresh coriander leaves, to serve (optional)

SAFFRON BASMATI RICE
250g basmati rice (preferably brown)
Good pinch of saffron threads
Sea salt and freshly ground black pepper

Put 1 tablespoon of the oil in a large pan over a medium to high heat. Season the lamb with salt and pepper and then, working in batches, brown the lamb well, transferring it to a plate as you go. Working in batches ensures you don't overcrowd the pan, which would cause the lamb to sweat rather than brown.

Next, add the second tablespoon of oil to the pan, if necessary, and cook the onion for 6–8 minutes or until it is just beginning to go brown. Then add the bay leaves (just scrunch them to break them up a bit), cardamom pods, cloves, cinnamon, coriander, cumin, paprika and garam masala and cook for a minute or two until they just start to release their aromas.

Meanwhile, blitz the yogurt with the ginger and garlic in a mini blender until fairly smooth and then add this to the pan along with the tinned tomatoes and tomato purée. Bring to the boil and then reduce to a simmer. Please note here that if you are using a low-fat yogurt, do not bring it to the boil, but just bring it to a simmer or else it may 'split' or curdle. Add the reserved lamb and let it simmer away gently for about 10–12 minutes, stirring occasionally, until the sauce has thickened and the meat is cooked through.

Whilst the Rogan Josh simmers, cook the rice according to the packet instructions. Put the saffron threads into a small bowl or egg cup with 3 tablespoons of hot water and set aside to infuse. A few minutes before the rice is ready, tip the saffron mixture into the rice, season with a bit of salt and pepper and continue to cook until done.

Once the rice is ready, drain it if necessary and then divide among four plates. Season the Rogan Josh to taste and spoon on top of the rice. Sprinkle with coriander leaves, if using, and serve.

BEEF, BRANDY AND WILD MUSHROOM STROGANOFF

SERVES
4

This is a posh stroganoff. I have used sirloin or rump, but the quick-fry beef steaks you can buy are just as good and cheaper. Just make sure they are not too thin or the dish will not feel as succulent. It is always trial and error with how much flavour you want to put into a dish, so if you want more of a flavour punch, just add a little extra Worcestershire sauce and paprika.

2 tbsp sunflower oil
1 large onion, finely chopped
225g wild (or chestnut) mushrooms, wiped clean and sliced if large
3 fresh sage leaves, finely chopped (to give about 1 tsp)
1–2 tsp paprika
350g tagliatelle
3 x 200g sirloin or rump steaks, trimmed of fat and cut into bite-sized pieces
325ml good-quality beef stock
50ml brandy (or just omit altogether if you don't want any alcohol)
Good few shakes of Worcestershire sauce
100g crème fraîche (can use half-fat if you fancy it)
Leaves from ½ bunch of fresh parsley, very finely chopped (to give about 2 tbsp)
Sea salt and freshly ground black pepper

Heat 1 tablespoon of the oil in a large frying pan over a low to medium heat. Cook the onion for 4–5 minutes, stirring regularly, until just beginning to soften but not colour. Next, add the mushrooms and sage and paprika and continue to cook for 5 minutes until they begin to wilt. Tip this mixture into a medium bowl and set aside, reserving the frying pan too.

Put the pasta on to cook in a large pan of boiling, salted water according to the packet instructions until *al dente*.

Return the frying pan to a really high heat with the remaining tablespoon of oil and fry the steak pieces for 2–3 minutes, stirring regularly, or until they are brown all over. Tip them into the bowl with the mushroom mix.

Reduce to a high heat and add the stock, brandy and Worcestershire sauce. This will help deglaze the pan, so scrape any brown bits off the bottom with a wooden spoon for a minute as it bubbles. Season with salt and pepper and leave the liquid to bubble away and reduce down by about a third for 3–4 minutes. Then, reduce the heat to medium and return the meat and mushroom mix to the pan. Simmer for 2–3 minutes to heat through and then add the crème fraîche. Cook for a further minute, stirring. Season to taste, then stir the parsley through and remove from the heat.

Drain the cooked pasta well and divide amongst four serving plates. Spoon the stroganoff over and serve at once.

Top tip
If you are using half-fat crème fraîche, then do not let it boil as the crème fraîche will just curdle.

BUTTERFLIED ROSEMARY ROAST LEG OF LAMB WITH GINGER MINT SALSA ON A BED OF WATERCRESS

SERVES
8–10

As I am sure you know, butterflied leg of lamb just means that it has had the bone removed and so is now opened up (like a butterfly!). If you are lucky enough to have a high street local butcher, then ask him to butterfly it for you, but if not, I have recently seen them at the supermarket already butterflied, which is very handy as doing it yourself is not the easiest thing in the world! I like to serve this with new potatoes.

ROSEMARY ROAST LAMB
1.75kg butterflied leg of lamb, from about a 2.5kg leg (you can find it like this at the supermarket or your butcher can do it for you)
4 stalks of fresh rosemary, cut into 3cm pieces

GINGER MINT SALSA
50ml white wine vinegar
1 tsp sugar, preferably brown
Leaves from 2 bunches of fresh parsley, finely chopped
Leaves from 1 bunch of fresh mint, finely chopped
3 ripe tomatoes, diced
2 garlic cloves, finely chopped
3cm piece of fresh ginger, finely diced
1 tsp ground cumin

WATERCRESS
75g bag of watercress
2 tsp extra virgin olive oil (optional)
Flaked sea salt and freshly ground black pepper

Preheat the oven to 200°C, (fan 180°C), 400°F, Gas Mark 6.

Season both sides of the lamb with salt and pepper and then lay it out flat on a large baking tray, fat-side up. Using the point of a small sharp knife, make slits all over the top of the joint and then push the rosemary pieces into these holes. Place the lamb into the oven for 35–40 minutes until it is browned and caramelised on the outside, but still pink and tender on the inside.

Once the lamb is ready, remove it from the oven, cover loosely with tin foil and leave to rest for about 20 minutes. This is such a vital step; not only does it make the lamb juicier, it evens out the temperature of the meat and allows the juices to stay within the meat, rather than running out all over the plate as soon as you cut into it.

As the lamb rests, prepare the salsa. Place the vinegar in a medium bowl and stir in the sugar until dissolved. Toss in the remaining ingredients, season to taste with salt and pepper and set aside.

Scatter the watercress all over a large plate and drizzle with some oil, if you like. Slice up the rested meat and lay it on top of the watercress. Spoon over the ginger mint salsa and serve.

Top tip
This salsa can accompany many different dishes. Try adding it to wraps, drizzling over BBQ meats or mixing with crème fraîche for a delicious dip.

JERK PORK CHOPS WITH A PEAR AND PECAN PILAF AND AN ORANGE GINGER DRESSING

SERVES
4

These are great to cook indoors or out on the BBQ. If you do cook them inside, then open those windows and turn the extractor fan on as high as you can go because the chilli flakes tend to catch in the back of the throat ... a lot!

PEAR AND PECAN PILAF
200g quinoa
50g pecan nuts
75g bag of rocket
1 ripe pear, quartered, cored and cut into about 1cm cubes

JERK PORK CHOPS
1 tbsp allspice
1 tsp ground cinnamon
1 tsp ground coriander
1 tsp chilli flakes
Big pinch of freshly grated nutmeg
Leaves from 6 sprigs of fresh thyme
1 tbsp balsamic vinegar
1–2 tbsp sunflower oil
2 tsp soy sauce
4 x 150g pork chops
3 garlic cloves, very finely chopped

ORANGE GINGER DRESSING
3 tbsp extra virgin olive oil
1 tbsp balsamic vinegar
1 garlic clove, finely chopped
1cm piece of fresh ginger, peeled and finely grated
Zest of 1/2 orange
1 tbsp orange juice
2 tsp sugar
1/2 tsp English mustard powder
Sea salt and freshly ground black pepper

Put the quinoa on to cook according to the packet instructions.

Put a small pan (with no oil) on a low heat and toast the pecan nuts for a few minutes, tossing frequently, until just catching colour and releasing their aroma. Remove, roughly chop and set aside.

Toss the allspice, cinnamon, coriander, chilli flakes, nutmeg, thyme leaves and salt and pepper in a wide shallow dish. Add the balsamic, 1 tablespoon of the oil and the soy sauce and mix until well blended. Add the pork chops, turning to coat all over.

Get a griddle or frying pan nice and hot. If using a frying pan, then add the second tablespoon of oil to the pan. Add the pork chops and cook for about 5 minutes per side or until they are just cooked through, well caramelised and brown on the outside.

As the chops cook, mix together the dressing ingredients in a small bowl. Season to taste and set aside.

Once the quinoa is cooked, drain it well if necessary, tip it out onto a large tray and set it aside so that it cools down a bit.

Two minutes before the pork chops are ready, add the garlic to the pan also. Once the pork chops are ready, remove them from the pan onto a plate. Cover with tin foil and leave to rest for a few minutes whilst you assemble the rest of the dish.

Put the quinoa into a large bowl and add the pecans, rocket and pear. Mix them together gently, spoon out onto four serving plates and sit a rested pork chop on top of each one. Add any meat resting juices to the dressing, drizzle this over the pork and serve at once.

PORK LOIN STEAKS WITH A PLUM PINOT SAUCE AND STOVETOP SWEET POTATO DAUPHINOISE

SERVES
4

This started out as a dish with a healthy twist. But making a robust dauphinoise with sweet potatoes just did not seem to work well with semi-skimmed milk. So I called in the classic duo of whole milk and double cream. The plum Pinot sauce brings this all together for a very filling cold-weather dish.

SWEET POTATO DAUPHINOISE
Spray oil
800g sweet potatoes, washed and thinly sliced (feel free to peel before slicing, but lots of the goodness is in the skin!)
1 bunch of spring onions, finely sliced
5 fresh sage leaves, finely chopped (to give about 1 tbsp)
2 bay leaves, torn into bits
2 knobs of butter, broken into small pieces (optional)
250ml whole milk
250ml double cream
Pinch of ground cinnamon or allspice

PORK LOIN STEAKS
2 tbsp sunflower oil
4 x 200g pork loin steaks
2 shallots, finely chopped

PLUM AND PINOT SAUCE
200ml Pinot Noir or another fine red
200ml chicken stock
2 tbsp plum jam
½ tsp allspice
3 fresh sage leaves, finely chopped
Sea salt and freshly ground black pepper

Starting with the dauphinoise, spray a 20–23cm sauté pan with some oil (or line the base with parchment paper, making sure it does not come up over the sides of the pan). Arrange slices of potato in the pan, in overlapping layers, sprinkling spring onion, sage, bay leaf pieces, knobs of butter, if using, and salt and pepper between them as you go. Gradually pour over the milk and cream, and then sprinkle the top with cinnamon or allspice.

Place the pan on the hob over a medium heat. Once the milk starts to bubble, turn the heat down to low, put a circle of parchment paper directly on top of the potatoes, a piece of tin foil over the top of the pan, followed by the lid, and leave it to simmer away gently for 20–25 minutes.

Meanwhile get a large frying pan, with 1 tablespoon of oil, nice and hot over a high heat. Season the pork steaks, add to the pan and reduce the heat to medium. Continue to fry for 3–4 minutes on each side. They should be nicely browned. Once cooked, transfer them to a plate, cover with tin foil to keep warm and rest.

Add the second tablespoon of oil to the frying pan with the shallots, reduce the heat and cook gently for 3–4 minutes. Then add the wine and stock, scraping any sticky bits from the meat from the bottom of the pan. Turn up the heat and bubble away for 5–6 minutes or until the mixture has reduced by a third. Then add the plum jam, allspice and sage and any resting juices from the meat and cook for a couple more minutes until reduced and thickened, and then set aside.

Check that the sweet potatoes are cooked through by piercing a knife through. Spoon the dauphinoise into four serving plates, sit a pork loin on top, drizzle the sauce over and serve at once.

SLOW-COOKER ASIAN PULLED PORK WITH GINGER, FIVE-SPICE AND SOY AND SPICY SLAW

SERVES
10–12

I like to serve my Asian pulled pork in toasted buns, preferably those with some sesame seeds on top, with a smear of mayonnaise. It makes a nice change from always having rice with this, and my daughter, as long as I go easy on the chilli, really loves it! This is great for entertaining a hungry crowd.

ASIAN PULLED PORK
5 tbsp soy sauce
4 tbsp mild or hot chilli powder
3 tbsp five-spice powder
2 tbsp light muscovado sugar
2 garlic cloves, finely chopped
4cm piece of fresh ginger, peeled and finely chopped
3kg boneless pork shoulder, rind removed

SPICY SLAW
3 tbsp sesame oil
2 tbsp soy sauce
½ red cabbage, very finely sliced
1 red onion, finely chopped
1 large carrot, cut into thin matchsticks
2 red chillies, deseeded for less heat if preferred, finely chopped
Large handful of fresh coriander leaves (optional)
Freshly ground black pepper

TO SERVE
10–12 sesame seed buns, split open and toasted

EQUIPMENT
Large slow cooker

Place the soy sauce, chilli powder, five-spice, sugar, garlic and ginger in a large slow cooker and mix together well to give a sloppy paste. Sit the pork shoulder on top and massage the spice mixture well all over the meat. Put the lid on the slow cooker and cook on low for 8–10 hours, or until the meat is so tender you can shred it with a fork.

Close to serving time, make the slaw. Mix the sesame oil and soy sauce together in a large bowl. Toss the cabbage, onion, carrot, chilli and coriander, if using, through until well mixed. Season to taste with pepper.

Once the pork is ready, shred it with a fork and serve. It is delicious piled into toasted sesame buns with the spicy slaw. If you would like to serve it with a sauce, then bubble the cooking juices in a large wide pan on a high heat for 10–15 minutes until reduced and thickened slightly. Season to taste with pepper.

BE SELECTIVE IN YOUR BATTLES; SOMETIMES
PEACE IS BETTER THAN BEING RIGHT.

RITU GHATOUREY

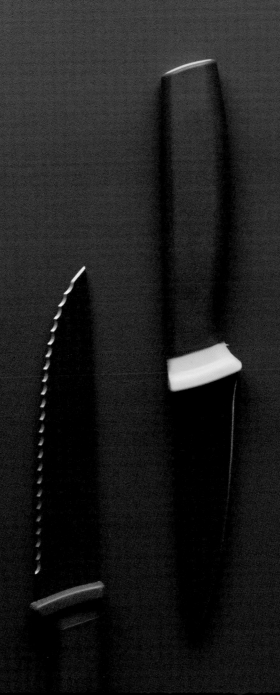

MAINS: FISH & SHELLFISH

SESAME AND SZECHUAN-COATED SEARED TUNA STEAK WITH CORIANDER, MANGO AND CHILLI GUACAMOLE 'SALSA'

SERVES
4

I do love a quick-cook dinner/lunch dish. Szechuan peppercorns are curious things, which leave the tongue tingling after eating. Not for everyone, but my family just love them. Serve this with a good squeeze of lime or a drizzle of soy sauce along with the guacamole salsa.

SESAME AND SZECHUAN TUNA
50g sesame seeds
1 tbsp Szechuan peppercorns, very finely ground
4 x 175–200g sustainably caught tuna steaks
Spray oil
75g bag of rocket

CORIANDER, MANGO AND CHILLI GUACAMOLE 'SALSA'
3 perfectly ripe avocados
Juice of 1 lime
1 bunch of spring onions, finely sliced
1 perfectly ripe mango, peeled, de-stoned and chopped into small chunks (to give about 250g flesh)
3 medium tomatoes, finely diced
2 red chillies, deseeded for less heat if preferred, finely sliced
Leaves from 1 large bunch of fresh coriander, roughly chopped
2cm piece of fresh ginger, peeled and finely grated (optional)
Sea salt and freshly ground black pepper

TO SERVE
A little soy sauce or a good squeeze of lime

Toss the sesame seeds, ground Szechuan peppercorns and a little salt and pepper together on a large flat plate and spread the mix out in an even layer. Spray the tuna steaks with a little oil and rub them all over to evenly coat. Press each side of the tuna steaks into the sesame mix until evenly coated. Then leave on the plate, cover with cling film, and place in the fridge for 10 minutes or so for the seeds to set on the steaks.

Meanwhile, make the guacamole. Cut the avocados in half, remove the stone and scoop the flesh out into a large bowl. Add the lime juice and mash the avocado well with a fork. Then gently stir through the spring onion, mango, tomato, chilli, coriander and ginger, if using. Season to taste with salt and pepper and set aside whilst you cook the tuna.

Spray a little oil into a large frying pan (or two if you don't think your four tuna steaks will fit in one) and get it nice and hot on a medium to high heat. Remove the tuna steaks from the fridge and cook them for 2–3 minutes per side until the outside is golden and the inside still a little pink.

Transfer each tuna steak to a serving plate and divide the rocket evenly among them. Spoon a dollop of guacamole beside each piece of tuna and serve at once with a little soy sauce or a good squeeze of lime for the tuna.

CRISPY SKIN SALMON WITH POLENTA CHIPS WRAPPED IN PANCETTA SERVED WITH ASPARAGUS AND GREMOLATA

SERVES
4

When buying salmon look for the MSC label, which means that the salmon is from a sustainable source. Polenta (cornmeal) is rather strange-looking stuff and the instant kind, when boiled up, looks rather like mashed potato. However, when set into a square and cut into 'chips', it starts to turn into something rather special.

POLENTA CHIPS
900ml good-quality vegetable or chicken stock
200g instant polenta
1 stalk of fresh rosemary, leaves finely chopped (to give about 1 tbsp)
20 large fresh sage leaves
20 slices of pancetta
2 tbsp olive oil

GREMOLATA
4 garlic cloves (can use more or less depending on your taste), roughly chopped
Handful of fresh parsley, roughly chopped
Finely grated zest of 1 lemon
50ml olive oil

CRISPY SKIN SALMON
2 tbsp olive oil
4 sustainably caught salmon steaks, with the skin scored
1 lemon, cut into wedges, to serve
Flaked sea salt and freshly ground black pepper

ASPARAGUS
1 tbsp olive oil
250g asparagus spears

SAUCE (OPTIONAL)
50g unsalted butter
Small handful of fresh parsley leaves, finely chopped
Juice of 1 lemon

EQUIPMENT
20cm square tin

Line a 20cm square tin with baking parchment or heatproof cling film. Bring the stock to the boil in a large saucepan. Reduce the heat to a fast simmer and, using a silicone whisk or rubber spatula, gradually stir in the polenta. Add the rosemary and season with salt and pepper. Cook for 4–5 minutes, stirring constantly, until large volcanic-like bubbles form. The polenta will swell and become really thick. Remove immediately or it could become lumpy. Pour the mixture into the prepared tin and smooth the surface with the back of a spoon. Set aside to cool for 20 minutes.

Meanwhile, make the gremolata. Place the garlic, parsley and lemon zest in a pestle and mortar and pound the mixture to a mash so all the flavours mix together. Then stir the oil through. Alternatively, blend everything together in a mini blender until as fine as possible. Either way, spoon into a small serving bowl and set aside.

Line a large baking sheet with baking parchment. Once the polenta is firm, pull it up out of the tin, place on a chopping board and carefully remove the paper or cling film. Cut the slab into 10 x 2cm wide strips and then cut them in half across to give twenty chunky chips. Being careful not to break the chips, wrap a sage leaf around the middle of each one, followed by a slice of pancetta. Arrange on the tray as you go. These can be prepared to this stage a day ahead of time, in which case, cover with cling film and keep in the fridge. ≫

Preheat the oven to 110°C, (fan 80°C), 225°F, Gas Mark ¼.
Heat two large frying pans on a medium to high heat and drizzle a tablespoon of oil into each one. Fry ten polenta chips in each pan for about 1–2 minutes on each side. Use a small fish slice to carefully turn the chips over to avoid breaking them. Arrange them back on the baking sheet once cooked and pop in the oven to keep warm.

Wipe out the frying pans with kitchen paper and return both to a medium to high heat with a tablespoon of oil in each one. Season the salmon with salt and pepper and once the oil is hot, place the fish skin-side down in one pan and leave to cook for about 3–4 minutes.

Meanwhile, sauté the asparagus in the oil in the other pan for 3–4 minutes, tossing occasionally.

If you want to make the sauce, simply melt the butter in a small saucepan, add the finely chopped parsley and lemon juice and season to taste.

Once the fish has had its time, flip it over and let it cook for 4 minutes on the other side.

Meanwhile, remove the polenta chips from the oven and arrange five on each serving plate. Divide the asparagus evenly among them also. Once the salmon is cooked to your liking (either a little pink in the centre or cooked completely through) remove from the heat and arrange one on each serving plate. If you made the optional sauce, pour this over now. Serve at once with the gremolata and lemon wedges.

Top tip
Trout would also work well for this very good-looking dish.

PAN-FRIED SALMON WITH BROCCOLI, PEAS AND CHILLI WITH A WARM MAPLE, ORANGE AND GINGER DRESSING

SERVES
4

This recipe is a little bit 'pantastic', using a total of three pans in one go! The dish would also be lovely as a salad. Mix everything together except the salmon and then just flake the salmon in afterwards. I have to say it ... Yumsters.

1 tbsp sunflower oil
4 x 175g sustainably caught salmon fillets
1 whole head of broccoli (about 400g), broken into bite-sized pieces
200g frozen peas
1–2 chillies, deseeded for less heat if preferred, finely sliced
Leaves from ½ x 28g bag of fresh mint
Handful of toasted flaked almonds (optional)

MAPLE, ORANGE AND GINGER DRESSING
2 tbsp extra virgin olive oil
1–2 tbsp maple syrup, to taste
2cm piece of fresh ginger, peeled and very finely chopped
Finely grated zest and juice of 1 orange
Sea salt and freshly ground black pepper

Bring a medium pan of salted water to the boil over a high heat (for the broccoli).

Put the oil in a large frying pan and place on the hob over a medium to high heat. Season the salmon fillets with a little salt and pepper and place them in, skin-side down first. Leave to cook for 3–4 minutes, without moving.

Meanwhile, cook the broccoli in the boiling water for 3 minutes. Then add the frozen peas, put a lid on to bring it all back to the boil quickly, then once boiling, remove the lid and boil for 3 more minutes.

Turn the salmon fillets over to cook on the opposite side for a further 3–4 minutes, or as liked.

Whilst these both cook, put all of the dressing ingredients into a small pan with a little salt and pepper. Bring to the boil over a high heat and then leave to bubble away for 2–3 minutes before removing and setting aside.

Drain the vegetables well and tip them back into the pan. Toss the chillies through and then divide among the four serving plates. Once the salmon is cooked just how you like it (I find 3–4 minutes per side is perfect), lay it on top of the veg, pour over the dressing, rip over the mint leaves and scatter over the almonds, if using, and serve.

QUICK LINGUINE WITH PRAWNS, CLAMS, GARLIC AND CHILLI

SERVES
4

350g dried linguine or spaghetti (regular or wholewheat)
3 tbsp extra virgin olive oil, plus extra for drizzling
2 large banana shallots, finely diced
3 garlic cloves, very finely chopped
2 red chillies, deseeded for less heat if preferred, finely chopped
400g sustainably caught raw peeled tiger prawns, de-veined
400g clams in their shells, washed thoroughly
1 glass of white wine (about 150–200ml)
1 small bunch of fresh parsley, roughly chopped (to give about 3 tbsp)
70g bag of rocket
1 small lemon, cut into 4 wedges
Flaked sea salt and freshly ground black pepper

If buying frozen prawns, then buy more in weight than the recipe says to allow for the water content of the pack. You might need about 600g frozen prawns to yield the 400g defrosted prawns required here. People often tell me that cooking with shellfish is something that they find intimidating, so I have devised this dish to make the task a little easier. It is really a case of just bunging the shellfish into the pan, then standing back and letting the hob do the work for you.

Cook the pasta in a large saucepan of boiling water according to the packet instructions until *al dente*. I add a little salt to flavour and some oil to stop the pasta sticking, but this is optional.

Meanwhile, put the oil in a large saucepan (that has a tight-fitting lid) over a medium heat. Add the shallots and allow to sweat down for 8–10 minutes until softened, stirring from time to time. Add the garlic and chilli and cook for a couple of minutes.

Add the prawns and cook for 1 minute, stirring. Then add the clams and white wine, bring to the boil and then cover with a lid. Allow to cook for 4–5 minutes until the clam shells have all opened (discard any that don't) and the prawns have turned from grey to pink.

Once the pasta is cooked, drain well, tip it in on top of the shellfish and mix together well. Toss the chopped parsley through and season to taste.

Pile into serving bowls, drizzle with an extra bit of olive oil, scatter the rocket over, top with a good grinding of black pepper and serve each with a wedge of lemon.

Top tip
To prepare the clams, I usually soak them in cold water for 1 hour to get the sand out and discard any that remain open when tapped.

PRAWN, SWEET POTATO AND LIME CURRY WITH CHILLI AND BLACK PEPPER ROTI BREAD

SERVES
4

This curry is extremely tangy, full of flavour and pretty filling. The chilli and black pepper roti bread are kind of like naan bread, fun and quick to make and great to dip into the curry. I would definitely say this is a dish you could easily make when you come home from work. Fast, tasty, easy.

CHILLI AND BLACK PEPPER ROTI BREAD
200g plain flour (or a mixture of 50g wholemeal flour and 150g plain flour), plus extra for dusting
4 tsp baking powder
1–2 tsp chilli flakes (depending on how hot you like your chilli!)
1 tsp freshly ground black pepper
1 tsp fine sea salt
4 tsp sunflower oil

PRAWN, SWEET POTATO AND LIME CURRY
2 tsp desiccated coconut
2 tbsp medium or hot curry powder
2 sweet potatoes, peeled and cut into 1cm cubes
4cm piece of fresh ginger, peeled and cut into long thin strips
1/5 of a Scotch bonnet pepper or 1 red chilli, deseeded for less heat if preferred, finely chopped
400ml tin of coconut milk
250ml vegetable stock
75g sugar snap peas
75g baby corn, halved lengthways
225g sustainably caught, raw peeled jumbo king prawns, de-veined (defrosted if frozen)
1 bunch of spring onions, trimmed and sliced
Juice of 1 lime

First, make the roti bread. Put the flour(s), baking powder, chilli flakes, black pepper and salt in a large bowl. Toss together and make a well in the centre. Pour in 125ml cold water and mix everything together to give a nice soft dough. Knead the dough for 10 minutes by hand or 5 minutes in a freestanding electric mixer set with a dough hook and then set aside for a moment.

Preheat the oven to 110°C, (fan 90°C), 225°F, Gas Mark ¼. Put two large frying pans on the hob over a low to medium heat.

Divide the roti dough into four equal pieces and shape each one into a ball. Roll one out on a lightly floured surface until it is as thin as you can get it to give about an 18cm diameter circle. Then dust the top with a little more flour. Drizzle 1 teaspoon of oil into one pan and pop the dough disc in, leaving it to cook for about 2 minutes on each side.

Meanwhile, quickly roll out the second piece of dough in the same way. Drizzle another teaspoon of oil into the second pan and cook this roti in the same way. Once cooked, fold the roti in half, place on a small baking tray and pop into the oven to keep warm. Repeat until all the roti breads are cooked.

Next, put a large, dry sauté pan over a medium heat and toast the coconut for 2–3 minutes, tossing regularly, until it turns golden brown, and then tip into a bowl and set aside. ≫

PRAWN, SWEET POTATO AND LIME CURRY WITH CHILLI AND BLACK PEPPER ROTI BREAD

(continued)

Return the pan to a medium heat, add the curry powder and cook for about 2 minutes or so, tossing regularly, until you start to smell the aromas. Add the sweet potato, ginger and chilli and stir well. Then add the coconut milk and stock and cook, stirring, for a couple of minutes until it comes to the boil. Turn down the heat and simmer for about 6–8 minutes until the sweet potato is almost tender.

Next, add the sugar snaps and baby corn and cook for 4–6 minutes until tender, stirring occasionally. Add the prawns and cook for 2 minutes until they turn from grey to pink. Remove from the heat, throw in the spring onion, squeeze in the lime juice and season to taste.

Spoon into serving bowls, scatter the coconut over and serve with the warm roti breads.

ALMOND-CRUSTED COD WITH DILL SAUCE

SERVES
4

Dill is not everyone's favourite, so please feel free to serve it without. I did not love dill until a couple of years back and now I embrace its unusual flavour with things like fish and eggs. The crust gives welcome crunch and flavour to the not-so-powerfully flavoured cod.

DILL SAUCE
350g no-fat Greek yogurt
2 tbsp chopped fresh dill
Juice of ½ lime

ALMOND-CRUSTED COD
200g almonds
2 tbsp plain flour
2 stalks fresh rosemary, very finely chopped (or 1 tsp dried rosemary, thyme or mixed herbs)
4 sustainably caught cod or pollack fillets (make sure they carry the MSC symbol)
Spray oil
Flaked sea salt and freshly ground black pepper

Preheat the oven to 200°C, (fan 180°C), 400°F, Gas Mark 6.

Gently mix all of the dill sauce ingredients together, then season to taste, cover and pop in the fridge whilst you make your fish.

Line a large roasting tray with tin foil. Put the almonds into a food processor with the flour and rosemary or dried herbs and blitz. You do not want a powder, but something that is nice and coarse so you still get some texture once the fish is cooked. Once it is blitzed, tip it onto a plate and season with salt and pepper.

Cut the fish fillets into large fish fingers across the narrow part rather than from tail to top.

Spray a fish stick with oil and then dip it into the almonds. Make sure the fish stick is well covered and then place it into the roasting tin. Repeat with the rest of the fish sticks. Spray the top with a little more oil and then place in the oven for 10–12 minutes or until the fish is cooked through and the nuts are beginning to turn golden brown.

BAKED MISO-MARINATED SALMON WITH A CUCUMBER, CARROT AND SESAME SALAD AND CHILLI TOPPING

SERVES
4

Something new and different for your salmon. I eat salmon a lot and am always looking for new ways to serve it. This miso provides a punchy flavour and the cucumber and carrot salad looks happy on the plate.

BAKED MISO-MARINATED SALMON
4 sustainably caught salmon fillets
8 tbsp miso paste (you can find this in most big supermarkets)
4 tbsp white wine
4 tbsp brown sugar
4 tbsp mirin (you can find this in most big supermarkets)

CUCUMBER AND SESAME SALAD
2 cucumbers
4 carrots
2 tbsp sesame seeds
6 tbsp rice vinegar
Squidge of honey
Flaked sea salt and freshly ground black pepper

TOPPING
4 spring onions, very finely sliced on the diagonal
2 red chillis, thinly sliced

Put the salmon fillets into a large bowl, add the miso paste, white wine, brown sugar and mirin and mix together well. Set this aside for the flavours to infuse the fish for a minimum of 20 minutes and a maximum of overnight. I never get the timing right on this one and forget to do it overnight, so if you can chuck everything together just before you go to work the day you need it, then that should be fine.

Once the salmon has marinated, preheat the oven to 200°C, (fan 180°C), 400°F, Gas Mark 6. Scrape the marinade off the fish using the back of a knife or some kitchen towel. Place the fish on a tray lined with baking parchment and then bake for around 10–12 minutes depending on the size of the fish.

Whilst this is cooking, prepare your salad. Using a vegetable peeler, peel the cucumber in long strips from top to tail. Keep going until it becomes too fiddly to do so and then flip the cucumber over and start peeling that side. There will always be a bit in the middle that is just too hard to do. I usually just eat that bit as I make the rest of the dish!

Repeat with the carrot.

Put the cucumber and carrot into a bowl and add the sesame seeds, rice vinegar, a squidge of honey and some salt and pepper, mix and then leave to sit for a few moments.

Once the fish is cooked, remove it from the oven. Divide the salad between two plates, place the fish beside it, scatter over the spring onion and chilli and then serve.

LISTEN TO YOUR OWN VOICE. YOUR OWN SOUL.
IF SOMETHING DOES NOT FEEL RIGHT,
IT PROBABLY ISN'T.

UNKNOWN

VEGETABLES & SIDES

CHARGRILLED CORN ON THE COB WITH GARLIC BUTTER AND CORIANDER

SERVES
4 (or 8 if halved)

4 corn on the cob, whole or halved
1 tbsp sunflower oil
60g butter
1–2 garlic cloves, very,
    very finely chopped
1 medium red chilli,
    very finely chopped
1 handful of finely chopped
    fresh coriander
Flaked sea salt and freshly ground
    black pepper

I know most of you know how to do a corn on the cob. I remember Mum making corn on the cob, throwing it in some water, bringing it up to the boil. Let it bubble away a little bit, drain, and then serve with loads of butter. And, oh yes, that is very much good enough. But last summer, I took these golden bullets of corn, boiled them and finished them off on the BBQ and oh, what a difference a bit of toastiness makes. You don't have to drag out your possibly cobwebbed BBQ from the end of the garden; I have grilled these instead to equally tasty effect. To spice things up a bit, serve with chopped red chilli and sprinkle with some coriander for extra bite and freshness.

Put a large pan of water on to boil with a pinch of salt. I pop the lid on as the water is coming to the boil, which makes the water heat up much faster.

Once the water is boiling, remove the lid and add the corn and let this bubble away for 5 minutes. As this cooks, get the grill on really nice and hot (alternatively, you can cook the cobs on a griddle pan).

Once the cobs have cooked for 5 minutes, remove them from the heat and drain well, dab with some kitchen towel to remove excess moisture and brush all over with the oil. Arrange on a grill rack and place them under the grill (or on a hot griddle pan, if using). Cook them for 6–8 minutes, turning them from time to time so they catch a good and even colour.

As they cook, melt the butter over a low heat in the pan the corn was boiled in. Stir the garlic and chilli in with salt and pepper, cook for 1 minute, and then set the pan aside.

Once the cobs have a good colour, remove them from the grill (or pan). Toss them in the garlic butter and then stick a corn-on-the-cob holder in each end of each cob. Arrange them on serving plates, drizzling over any remaining butter from the pan, then sprinkle over the coriander and serve.

ROASTED BEETROOT AND APPLE WITH TOASTED PUMPKIN SEEDS

SERVES
4–6

I have been trying to make my vegetable accompaniments more interesting. It is so tempting to just take the easy route and chuck some peas (much as I love peas) into a pan to serve with things. Roasting beetroots gives them a softer flavour and the apples give a subtle sweetness to this dish. I serve this with a roast or just cook it to have as an on-the-go salad with some grilled chicken for lunch.

8 medium-large fresh beetroots, trimmed, peeled and quartered
4 garlic cloves, peeled
2 tbsp olive oil
2 apples, peeled, quartered and cored
Large handful of pumpkin seeds (about 25g)
1 tbsp cumin seeds
4 tbsp extra virgin olive oil
3 tbsp balsamic vinegar
Squidge of honey
Leaves from 1 bunch of fresh mint, finely sliced (to give about 4 tbsp)
Sea salt and freshly ground black pepper

Preheat the oven to 200°C, (fan 180°C), 400°F, Gas Mark 6.

Toss the beetroot, garlic and oil together on a roasting tray and season well with salt and pepper. Roast in the oven for about 45 minutes–1 hour (depending on their size) or until soft through when pierced with a sharp knife. Add the apple and pumpkin seeds after 25 minutes, tossing them through the beetroot.

Meanwhile, put the cumin seeds in a frying pan with no oil over a medium heat. Cook for 2–3 minutes until they begin to toast and become fragrant. Remove from the heat, tip them into a pestle and mortar and crush to a quite fine powder. Tip this into a mug and add the oil, balsamic vinegar, honey and salt and pepper. Whisk up really well and then set aside.

Once the beetroot and apple are soft, remove them from the oven. Whisk up the cumin dressing again and pour this over the veg. Tip everything onto a large platter, scatter over the mint and serve.

CRISPY ROASTED CABBAGE WITH A WARM PECAN AND THYME DRESSING

SERVES
6–8

Cabbage to me is a bit blah, a bit ordinary and sometimes stinky, and I am not so much a fan of coleslaw. But when in doubt with a veg, it often works when roasted and so that is exactly what I did with this. Roasting cabbage really turns the flavour around and the warm pecan and thyme dressing just makes it extra yum. I like to serve this with a roast for the perfect veggie/meat match.

4 baby cabbages or 1 large white cabbage
Spray oil or 1 tbsp olive oil
Sea salt and freshly ground black pepper

PECAN AND THYME DRESSING

12 pecan nuts, roughly chopped
4 tbsp extra virgin olive oil
2 tbsp cider vinegar or balsamic vinegar
Leaves from 4 fresh thyme sprigs, roughly chopped (to give about 1 tbsp)

Preheat the oven to 200°C, (fan 180°C), 400°F, Gas Mark 6.

Leaving the cabbage(s) whole, carefully cut into 1cm thick slices, arranging them lying flat on two large baking sheets as you go. Spray or brush the oil over them and scatter with salt and pepper. Roast in the oven for 30 minutes or until the cabbage starts to go a little brown and crispy at the edges. Swap the trays around halfway through cooking.

Five minutes before the cabbage is ready, put the pecan nuts in a small dry frying pan on a medium heat and cook for 2–3 minutes to really bring the flavours out. Keep the pan moving so they do not burn. Remove from the heat and add the oil, vinegar and thyme, allowing them to bubble in the residual heat. Set aside.

Once cooked, remove the cabbage from the oven, pour over the warm dressing and serve at once.

GRIDDLED AUBERGINE WITH TOASTED CASHEWS, GRUYÈRE AND A BASIL AND LEMON CHIMICHURRI

SERVES
4–6

When I first ate aubergines I thought they tasted like smoky tea bags and vowed never to have them again. But after having swallowed those words, I have tried them in many restaurants and have since developed a taste for them. I am mishmashing all sorts of flavours together here, but they really do work. The crunch and sweetness of the cashews, the slight saltiness and sweetness of the Gruyère and the acidity and fragrance of the basil and lemon chimichurri with the smoky aubergine are a powerful combination. Here they are griddled, but you can also pop them under the grill.

2 tsp coriander seeds
3 large aubergines, trimmed
Spray oil or 2 tbsp extra virgin olive oil
50g unsalted cashew nuts, roughly chopped
25g Gruyère cheese

BASIL AND LEMON CHIMICHURRI
75ml extra virgin olive oil
Leaves from 2 bunches of fresh basil (to give about 50g)
2 garlic cloves, roughly chopped
1 red chilli, deseeded for less heat if preferred, roughly chopped
Juice of ½ lemon
Sea salt and freshly ground black pepper

Toast the coriander seeds in a small dry frying pan on a low to medium heat for 2–3 minutes until toasted and fragrant. Tip into a pestle and mortar, roughly grind, stir in a little salt and pepper and then set aside.

Get a large griddle pan (or a frying pan will work well also) really nice and hot on a high heat. Depending on its size, you may need two, or alternatively you can cook the aubergines in batches. Cut the aubergines into quarters lengthwise and spray or brush the cut sides with oil. Sprinkle the crushed coriander seeds evenly over to stick. Cook the aubergine pieces on each (of the two) cut sides for 3–4 minutes until nicely charred.

Meanwhile, toast the cashew nuts in a small dry frying pan on a low to medium heat for 2–3 minutes until just turning golden. Remove and pour into a small bowl or plate and set aside.

Put the chimichurri ingredients into a blender and blitz to a rough paste. Season to taste and set aside.

Once the cut sides of the aubergines are well charred, flip them over to the skin side and cook for a couple of minutes more. Transfer them onto a large serving platter and drizzle the chimichurri over. Scatter the cashew nuts on top, shave the Gruyère cheese over with a vegetable peeler and serve.

Top tip
Chimichurri is incredibly versatile; use as a marinade for meat, fish and veg; use as a dipping sauce for kebabs on the BBQ, or stir through roasted vegetables. The possibilities are endless!

PAN-FRIED KALE WITH POMEGRANATE AND FETA WITH A CHILLI HONEY DRESSING

SERVES
2–4 (as a lunch)

A really lovely colourful side.

200g kale
Spray oil
Leaves from 3 sprigs of
    fresh thyme
200g feta, drained
1 pack of pomegranate seeds or
    the seeds of 1 pomegranate

CHILLI HONEY DRESSING
3 tbsp extra virgin olive oil
2 tsp red wine vinegar
Good pinch of chilli flakes
    (or 1 small chilli, deseeded
    and very finely chopped)
Tiny squidge of honey (optional,
    but I like to put it in)
Sea salt and freshly ground
    black pepper

To prepare the kale, rip out any stalks, tear the leaves into slightly smaller pieces, rinse them in cold water and drain well.

Spray a little oil in the bottom of a large sauté pan or wok and place over a medium heat. Add the kale, thyme and a little salt and pepper and cook for 5–6 minutes, tossing regularly.

As this cooks, make the dressing. Place the oil, vinegar, chilli flakes to taste, or fresh chilli, and honey, if using, in a mug and whisk up well with a fork. Season to taste with salt and pepper and set aside.

The kale should be soft and wilted once cooked. Toss the dressing through to evenly coat. Remove from the heat and tip into a large, wide serving bowl. Crumble over the feta, scatter with pomegranate seeds and serve.

CHESTNUT AND MUSHROOM BOURGUIGNON WITH ROSEMARY AND THYME AND CHIVE MASHED POTATOES

SERVES
4

This book has a real mix of light and hearty recipes to try to give you something to cook no matter what the weather or your mood. This rib-sticking dish should be cooked in a red wine from Burgundy, but do use whichever red wine you can get your hands on – and the more robust the better.

CHESTNUT AND MUSHROOM BOURGUIGNON

2 tbsp sunflower oil
1 large carrot, finely cubed
1 stick of celery, finely cubed
Leaves from 2 stalks of fresh rosemary, finely chopped (to give about 1 tbsp)
Leaves from 8 sprigs of fresh thyme (to give about 2 tbsp)
1 bay leaf
2–3 garlic cloves, finely chopped
2 tbsp plain flour
1 large glass of red wine (about 175ml)
1 litre vegetable or chicken stock
2 tbsp tomato purée
900g chestnut mushrooms, quartered
8 shallots or small onions, peeled
250g cooked, peeled chestnuts (from a vac pac or can)
1 tbsp finely chopped fresh flat-leaf parsley, to serve (optional)

ROSEMARY AND THYME MASHED POTATOES

4 large jacket potatoes
50g butter
Bunch of fresh chives, finely chopped (optional)
Pinch of freshly grated nutmeg (optional)
Sea salt and freshly ground black pepper

Preheat the oven to 200°C, (fan 180°C), 400°F, Gas Mark 6.

Prick the potatoes with a fork and rub them with a little of the butter. Then wrap them in tin foil and pop them in the oven for about 1 hour.

About 40 minutes before the potatoes are ready, start cooking the bourguignon. Heat the oil in a large pan over a medium heat. Add the carrot, celery, rosemary, thyme and bay leaf and cook for 4–5 minutes until the vegetables are just beginning to soften. Next, stir in the garlic and flour and cook for 1 more minute. Turn the heat up to high, pour in the red wine, stirring to blend the flour in well, and let it bubble away for 2–3 minutes until thickened. Then, stir in the stock and tomato purée, followed by the mushrooms and shallots. Bring to the boil and then reduce to simmer for a good 20 minutes until thickened. Add the chestnuts, season to taste with salt and pepper and cook for another 5 minutes to heat through. ≫

CHESTNUT AND MUSHROOM BOURGUIGNON WITH ROSEMARY AND THYME AND CHIVE MASHED POTATOES

(continued)

Once the potatoes feel tender when pierced with a knife, remove them from the oven. Split them open and scrape out their fluffy insides into a medium bowl. Add the remaining butter, chives and nutmeg, if using, and season with salt and pepper, and then mash everything well. Alternatively, you can just serve the potatoes split down the middle.

Spoon the mash onto each serving plate and ladle the bourguignon over. Sprinkle with chopped parsley to serve, if you like.

Top tip
For a slightly sweeter and deeper flavour, use port or Madeira instead.

Using a slow cooker: Obviously in this case you will need to have the mash pre-prepared to warm through quickly for serving or else pop the potatoes in to cook about an hour before the bourguignon is ready. The ingredients are the same except you only need 800ml stock (rather than 1 litre). Blend the flour into the port in a small bowl until smooth. Place this and all the remaining ingredients into a slow cooker and season with salt and pepper. Set it to low and leave to cook for 7–8 hours. When it is cooked, strain the bourguignon through a colander set over a wide sauté pan to catch the sauce. Keep the vegetables warm and bubble the sauce on a high heat for about 10 minutes until reduced and thickened. Stir everything back together and serve sprinkled with chopped parsley, if you like.

BAKED SWEET POTATOES STUFFED WITH A HOT BEAN AND LENTIL CHILLI WITH RED PEPPERS AND PORT

SERVES
4–6

I remember when there were Spudulike and potato shops on every high street. My favourite would be simply loads of butter and lots of cheese. Now we are trying to be more healthy, these potato shops seem to have disappeared. I think someone should do sweet potato shops instead, for a more modern and healthier alternative! To change things up a bit now and again, you could always serve this chilli with either pasta or rice instead.

4–6 large sweet potatoes, washed and dried
Spray oil or 1 tbsp sunflower oil
1 tbsp sunflower oil
1 large onion, finely chopped
2 large carrots, thinly sliced
2 tsp mild or hot chilli powder
2 tsp cayenne pepper
2 tsp ground cumin
2 red peppers, deseeded and cut into bite-sized chunks
2 red chillies, deseeded for less heat if preferred, sliced
2 garlic cloves, finely chopped
2 x 400g tins of chopped tomatoes
1 glass port or red wine or a good vegetable stock
75g tomato purée
400g tin of lentils, drained and rinsed
400g tin of kidney beans, drained and rinsed
198g tin of sweetcorn, drained
1 tsp sugar (optional)
4 tbsp crème fraîche
Leaves from 1 bunch of fresh coriander or flat-leaf parsley, roughly chopped (to give about 4 tbsp)
Flaked sea salt and freshly ground black pepper

Preheat the oven to 200°C, (fan 180°C), 400°F, Gas Mark 6.

Spray the sweet potatoes with some oil, prick them all over with a fork and place them on a baking tray. Once the oven is up to temperature, pop them in to bake for ¾–1 hour, depending on size.

Put the oil in a large pan over a low heat. Add the onion and carrot and cook for 8–10 minutes, stirring regularly, until soft but without colour. Stir in the chilli powder, cayenne and cumin and cook for 1 minute. Then stir in the peppers, chilli and garlic and cook for another minute. Add the tinned tomatoes, port (or wine or stock), tomato purée and salt and pepper. Then turn up the heat and bring to the boil, before reducing the heat to simmer for 5 minutes. Next, add the lentils, kidney beans and sweetcorn and leave to simmer for 6–8 minutes or until the vegetables are soft. Season to taste, but if you feel the chilli is still a bit tart from the tomatoes, then just add the sugar and cook through for a moment.

Once tender through to the centre when pierced with a knife, remove the sweet potatoes from the oven, slit them in half along their length and place two halves, cut-side up, on each serving plate. Top with the chilli, add a dollop of crème fraîche to each one, scatter the coriander or parsley over and serve straight away.

PAN-FRIED KALE WITH PEAR AND ROASTED HAZELNUTS AND MAPLE DRESSING

SERVES
4–6 (as a side dish)

A quick, simple side, great on its own or as an accompaniment to pork, chicken or veggies.

Spray oil
2 shallots, finely chopped
200g kale
2 perfectly ripe pears
1 tbsp extra virgin olive oil
2 tsp maple syrup
50g roasted hazelnuts (ready done from the supermarket)
Sea salt and freshly ground black pepper

Put a large wok on a medium heat and spray with some oil. Add the shallots along with a tablespoon of water and cook, stirring from time to time, for about 10 minutes or until the shallots have softened, but not coloured.

Meanwhile, to prepare the kale, rip out any stalks, tear the leaves into slightly smaller pieces, rinse them in cold water and drain well. Peel and quarter the pears, remove their cores and cut the flesh into bite-sized chunks.

Once the shallots have softened, add the kale, pear and a little salt and pepper and cook for 5–6 minutes, tossing regularly.

Meanwhile, prepare the dressing by simply mixing the olive oil and maple syrup in a mug with a fork. Season to taste and set aside.

Once the kale has wilted, pour over the dressing, tossing everything together well to combine. Remove from the heat, spoon into a large serving bowl, scatter over the roasted hazelnuts and serve immediately.

WHAT A WONDERFUL THOUGHT IT IS
THAT SOME OF THE BEST DAYS OF OUR
LIVES HAVE NOT HAPPENED YET.

UNKNOWN

DESSERTS, CAKES & TREATS

BAKED RICOTTA AND CREAM CHEESE CHEESECAKE WITH BLACKBERRIES, BLUEBERRIES AND FIGS

SERVES
8–10

In previous books I have done my cheesecakes without the need to put them in the oven. Partly due to laziness and partly because I was unsure of the taste. But through experimentation and the blessing of learning to be more patient, I finally succumbed and put a baked cheesecake in the book. I did try with the lower-fat cream cheese and it kind of worked, but the texture was very grainy and the cake did not look good, so full-fat cream cheese it is. A stunning cheesecake with so much rich, creamy flavour. I believe I am now a baked cheesecake expert!

50g unsalted butter
200g ginger nut biscuits (about 20 biscuits)
450g full-fat cream cheese
250g ricotta
150ml double cream
3 medium eggs
125g caster sugar
2½ tbsp cornflour
Seeds of 1 vanilla pod

125g fresh blueberries
125g fresh blackberries
2 figs, each cut into 6 even-sized wedges
2 tsp icing sugar, sifted
Handful of fresh mint leaves (optional)

EQUIPMENT
23cm springform cake tin

Preheat the oven to 170°C, (fan 150°C), 325°F, Gas Mark 3.

First, to make the base, put the butter on to melt in a medium saucepan over a low heat (or a bowl in the microwave). Line the base of a 23cm springform cake tin with baking parchment, brushing a little of the melted butter on the base to stick. Blitz up the ginger nut biscuits in a food processor to give fine crumbs. Mix well into the melted butter and then tip into the prepared tin. Press the mixture into the bottom so it is packed nice and tight and level, and then place in the fridge to set for 20 minutes or so whilst you get on with the filling.

Put the cream cheese, ricotta, cream, eggs, sugar, cornflour and vanilla seeds into a large bowl and beat like mad for a few minutes until everything is even and smooth. An electric mixer set with the whisk attachment will make this easier than doing it by hand.

Once the biscuit base is set, remove the tin from the fridge and pour this mixture on top. Sit on a baking tray and pop into the oven for 40–45 minutes. The cheesecake should be just set with a little wobble. When it reaches this stage, turn off the oven and leave to cool in there for about an hour. This (usually) stops the cheesecake from cracking. Avoiding moving the cheesecake around at this stage will help prevent cracking also. However, don't worry if it does crack as it will still taste delicious and will be nicely decorated.

Once the cheescake has had its hour of cooling, remove from the oven. The cheesecake may still be a little bit warm, so you can either eat it like this or wait and eat it when it is completely cool. Either way it is delicious! Arrange the berries and figs on top, dust with icing sugar and scatter over mint leaves, if using, and serve. This will keep for a couple of days, covered, in the fridge.

STEM GINGER AND APRICOT WHITE CHOCOLATE-DIPPED BISCOTTI

MAKES
22

When these were made during the shooting of *How to Be a Better Cook* and after the 'hero' shot had been taken – the shot when the camera shows them all piled up on a plate looking lovely – I turned my back for a second and the crew descended like savage dogs on our white-dipped Italian friends, leaving only crumbs on the plate. With the addition of wholemeal flour, these biccies have a nutty taste, even without nuts (I am often asked to do nut-free recipes). If you don't dip them in chocolate, you can put a few in a bag, tie with a ribbon and then give them away as presents, too.

150g self-raising flour, plus extra for dusting
50g wholemeal flour
100g dried apricots, finely chopped
75g soft light brown sugar
6 stem ginger balls (from a jar in syrup), roughly chopped
25g golden raisins
1 tsp bicarbonate of soda
1 tsp baking powder
1 tsp ground ginger
1 tsp mixed spice
Pinch of fine sea salt
2 eggs, lightly beaten
Seeds of 1 vanilla pod
200g white chocolate (optional, depending on whether or not you want to dip your biscuits)

Preheat the oven to 170°C, (fan 150°C), 325°F, Gas Mark 3 and line two large baking sheets with baking parchment.

Put the flours, apricots, sugar, stem ginger, raisins, bicarb, baking powder, ginger, mixed spice and salt in a bowl. Toss together and make a well in the centre. Add the eggs and vanilla seeds and mix everything together. As the mixture begins to come together in a lump it will look quite dry, but it will eventually form a ball.

Dust a clean work surface and your hands with a little self-raising flour, tip the ball out onto it and knead it for a minute or so until smooth. Then roll the ball out into a sausage shape about 30cm long and 5cm wide. Gently lift it up and place it on one of the baking sheets. Squash it down a little bit with the palm of your hands to flatten so it becomes about 8cm wide and 1.5cm high.

Place in the oven and bake for 30 minutes or until it is firm. A knife inserted into the centre of the biscotti should come out nice and clean. At this stage, remove it from the oven and then leave it to cool down until you can handle it. Gently slide the biscotti onto a chopping board (I use a fish slice to help with this) and use a sharp carving or bread knife to cut it into about 30 x 1.5cm wide, slightly slanted slices. Cut it really slowly as it will be quite crumbly. Arrange the slices lying down on both baking sheets as you go. Then place them back in the oven to bake for 40 minutes, turning them over halfway through the cooking time. »

When they are cooked, they should be very crisp and firm as they are twice-baked. Once cooked, remove from the oven and when cool enough to handle, transfer to a wire rack to cool completely. The chocolate dipping is an optional extra as these biscuits taste delicious without it too, so if you want to do the chocolate option, please follow the instructions below.

Once the biscotti are cool, break the white chocolate into a medium bowl and set over a pan of simmering water to slowly melt. Alternatively, melt in a bowl in the microwave in 30-second blasts. Either way, stir occasionally and remove once melted. Pour half the chocolate into a small bowl.

Hold a biscotti, base down, over one of the bowls of melted chocolate and dip the biscuit in so that just the base is covered, then allow the excess chocolate to drip off. Lay the biscotti back down on the tray and repeat with the remainder. Use the second bowl of chocolate once the first is used up. I like to use it in two separate batches as the crumbs from the biscotti tend to fall in and make the chocolate messy.

Once all coated, transfer the trays to the fridge for about 30 minutes to allow the chocolate to set. They can then be kept in an airtight container in a cool, dark place for up to a week.

Top tip
When working with white chocolate, if it gets lumpy and bumpy, just return it to the bain marie until it is smooth.

YOGURT AND VANILLA PANNA COTTA WITH RASPBERRY AND POMEGRANATE JELLY

SERVES
6

As I am sure you already know, a panna cotta is a cooked cream, usually set with gelatine. Gelatine contains animal products and so if you want, you may need to search further afield on your weekly shop for other setting agents such as agar, carrageen or kosher gelatine instead. I love the contrast of the white and the red (my favourite colour), but after you have tried this recipe once, if you fancy it, mix up the fruit the next time using mango or even blackberries for a different flavour. For a lighter dessert, in the past I have used low-fat Greek yogurt in place of the double cream and whole milk, which worked nicely. Not quite as creamy as using double cream, but far lighter on the tum.

YOGURT AND VANILLA PANNA COTTA
3 leaves of gelatine
100ml double cream
100ml whole milk
100g caster sugar
Seeds of 1 vanilla pod
300g Greek yogurt

RASPEBRRY AND POMEGRANATE JELLY
135g pack of raspberry jelly, cut into cubes
200ml just-boiled water
300ml pomegranate juice

TOPPING
Seeds from 1/2 pomegranate (optional)

EQUIPMENT
6 x 200ml pretty glasses

To make the panna cotta, put the gelatine in a bowl of cold water and leave to soak for 5 minutes.

Place the double cream, milk, sugar and vanilla seeds into a small pan and heat gently, just enough for the sugar to dissolve, stirring from time to time. Meanwhile, put the yogurt in a large jug, stirring to loosen, and set aside. Remove the creamy mixture from the heat once ready.

The gelatine should be soft by now, so lift it out of the water and squeeze the excess water out. Drop the gelatine into the creamy mixture and stir until dissolved. Leave to cool to body temperature for 10–15 minutes.

Meanwhile, prepare your glasses. As the layers are set at a slant, the glasses will need to be propped to one side. You may find egg cartons or even crumpled tea towels help prop the glasses. They could also tilt perfectly sitting in individual ramekins. Blu Tack may also come in handy! Whatever you use, set them on a large tray(s) that will easily fit in the fridge.

Once cool, pour the creamy mixture over the yogurt and then gently whisk everything together. Carefully pour the mixture into the six glasses, dividing it evenly. Carefully place the tray in the fridge and leave to set for 1–2 hours until firm. To set quickly, you can always whack them in the freezer for 20 minutes or so before popping them in the fridge to finish setting.

Meanwhile, for the jelly layer, place the raspberry jelly into a measuring jug. Pour over the boiling water and stir until the jelly dissolves. Stir in the pomegranate juice, then leave to cool at room temperature. If making this close to the time of adding the layer to the set panna cotta, then make sure it is really cool so as to not melt the panna cotta on impact.

Remove the set panna cottas from the fridge and stand the glasses upright. Pour the cool jelly over each one, dividing it evenly. Return to the fridge for about 2 hours until the jelly is set firm.

When you are ready to serve, top each one with pomegranate seeds, if using. These will keep for a few days in the fridge.

SUMMER PUDDING WITH SLIGHTLY DRUNKEN BERRIES AND WARM CHOCOLATE SAUCE

SERVES
8

I cannot bring myself to eat white soggy bread. In fact, I cannot bring myself to eat white sliced bread at the best of times (I am partial to a baguette though). With that in mind, and after my Twitter followers explained to me their dislike of the texture, I took a little culinary artistic licence with my summer pudding and am here using ready-cooked Madeira loaf, which due to its sweetness, bypasses the need to eat white bread at its worst. I hope you enjoy the frozen version, adding extra texture, slightly softened by the hot chocolate sauce.

175g soft light brown sugar
2 tbsp dark rum, port or a blackcurrant liqueur
Seeds of 1 vanilla pod (or a few drops of vanilla extract)
2 tsp ground cinnamon
2 tsp ground ginger
1kg fresh summer berries (I like a mixture of raspberries, blueberries, blackberries and redcurrants), stalks removed
2 ready-made Madeira loaf cakes
Small handful of fresh mint leaves, for decoration

WARM CHOCOLATE SAUCE
125ml double cream
100g dark chocolate (minimum 70% cocoa solids) or a mix of dark and milk if preferred, finely chopped
3 tbsp just-boiled water

EQUIPMENT
900g (2lb) loaf tin

Put the sugar in a large pan with 100ml water, place over a medium heat and stir until the sugar dissolves. Stir in the rum, port or blackcurrant liqueur, and vanilla seeds or extract and then turn up the heat and let it bubble away for 3–4 minutes to make a thin syrup. Turn down the heat to low and stir in the cinnamon and ginger. Reserve 250g of the berries for decoration, place about a quarter of the remainder in a separate bowl and then add the remainder to the pan, stirring them gently through. Leave to cook for 2 minutes until the fruit is soft, but still holding its shape. Remove from the heat and leave to cool for 20 minutes. The sauce should now be syrupy and look deep browny-red in colour and be very glossy.

Meanwhile, line a 900g (2 lb) loaf tin with a double layer of cling film, leaving excess hanging over the edge. Slice each Madeira cake into eight 2cm slices.

Stir the reserved quarter of berries gently into the cooled sauce. Tip the mixture into a large sieve over a medium bowl. Leave for 2 minutes to allow the syrup to drain through, but do not press as you don't want the fruit to become mushy. Sit the sieve on the pan so you can use the fruity syrup you have in the bowl for now.

Dip a slice of Madeira cake into the syrup, flip it over and then allow excess syrup to drip off. Place it against one of the long sides of the inside of the tin. Continue to dip the slices in the syrup and use three to four slices along each side of the tin in total. Place one on each end and then two to three slices along the bottom, breaking up to fit if necessary. Reserve the remaining slices for the top.

Tip the berries from the sieve into the cake-lined loaf tin, spreading them evenly. Add any syrup in the pan to the remaining syrup in the bowl and dip the remaining Madeira slices in to coat as before. Press the slices on top of the berries to completely cover. ≫

Reserve any remaining syrup in a covered bowl in the fridge for use later. Cover the loaf with the excess cling film and place a small baking tray or long plate on top. You can weigh the tray down with a couple of tins of food or something similar to help compress the fruit if you have room in your fridge, but it is not essential. Place in the fridge for about 6 hours or overnight until set firm.

About 10 minutes before serving, make the chocolate sauce. Put the cream in a medium pan over a medium heat and keeping a close eye on it, remove just before it comes to the boil. Break the chocolate into it and leave to sit and melt for 5 minutes before gently stirring together. Stir in the hot water to give a smooth, pourable consistency. Pour into a serving jug and keep warm.

Open out the cling film on the Madeira cake, turn a serving plate upside down on top of the loaf and turn both over. Remove the tin and peel off the cling film to reveal the pudding. Brush all over with the reserved syrup and decorate the top with the reserved berries and mint leaves. Serve at once with the chocolate sauce. The loaf can be cut into eight slices using a long, sharp knife.

JAMAICAN RUM TRUFFLES

MAKES
40

Super tasty, impressive, messy, but easy sweets. Omit the rum for the teetotallers amongst you and ramp up the rum to three tablespoons if you fancy the chocolates to have a good rum tang.

250ml whipping cream
100g milk chocolate,
    finely chopped
200g dark chocolate
    (minimum 70% cocoa solids),
    finely chopped
25g unsalted butter, diced
2–3 tbsp dark rum
5 tbsp cocoa powder, for dusting

Heat the cream in a small pan, removing it from the heat just before it comes to the boil. Put the chocolates in a large bowl and once the cream comes off the heat, pour it over the chocolate and stir well until melted and smooth. Add the butter and enough rum to taste and mix well. Leave to cool and then cover the chocolate mixture with cling film and pop in the fridge for 4 hours or overnight until set firm.

Line a large tray with baking parchment. Sift half the cocoa powder onto each of two large plates. One will be to dust your hands and the other to coat the truffles.

Use a teaspoon or melon baller to scoop up a walnut-sized piece (about 15g) of the truffle mixture. Press the palms of your hands into one of the cocoa powders to lightly coat and roll the truffle piece quickly into a ball. Don't roll it in your hands for too long or it will begin to melt.

Roll it around in the cocoa powder on the other plate to lightly coat and place on the tray. Repeat until all of the mixture is used up to give about forty truffles in total, pressing your hands into more cocoa powder when necessary to avoid sticking. It is best to wash your hands a few times throughout the process, but be sure to rinse them in cold water before drying so they are nice and cold to avoid melting the truffles.

Cover and chill in the fridge for at least 30 minutes before serving.

Top tip
These also freeze really well.

PUMPKIN, BROWN SUGAR AND PECAN CAKE WITH CREAM CHEESE ICING

SERVES
12

Naughty, rich and uber-tasty, this is a most unusual, but very satisfying cake.

400g pumpkin (or butternut squash), peeled, deseeded and coarsely grated (to give about 300g flesh)
350g self-raising flour
275g soft light brown sugar
1 large eating apple, peeled, cored and coarsely grated
2 tsp ground mixed spice
1 tsp ground cinnamon
1 tsp baking powder
1 tsp bicarbonate of soda
6 eggs
250ml vegetable oil, plus extra for greasing
Finely grated zest of 2 oranges
1 tsp vanilla extract

CREAM CHEESE ICING
300g low-fat cream cheese
3 tbsp icing sugar, sifted
Seeds of 1 vanilla pod

TO DECORATE
12 pecan nut halves

EQUIPMENT
Two 20cm sandwich tins

Preheat the oven to 190°C, (fan 170°C), 375°F, Gas Mark 5. Lightly grease the bottom of two 20cm sandwich tins, line with baking parchment and set on a baking tray.

Put the pumpkin, flour, sugar, apple, spices, baking powder and bicarb in a large bowl. Give them a quick toss together and then make a hole in the centre. Lightly beat the eggs in a medium bowl and then stir in the oil, orange zest and vanilla extract until combined. Pour the wet mixture into the dry ingredients and mix everything together until well combined.

Divide the mixture evenly between the two cake tins (they will be quite full) and place in the oven to bake for 40–45 minutes.

Meanwhile, prepare the icing by simply mixing the cream cheese, icing sugar and vanilla seeds together until smooth. Cover and chill in the fridge until ready to use.

To check the cakes are cooked, a skewer inserted into the centre of the cakes should come out clean. Once cooked, remove from the oven and leave to cool.

Once the sponges are cool, carefully remove them from the tins and place one of them on a serving plate or cake stand. Spread half of the cream cheese icing on top of this sponge. Place the other sponge on top and then spread the remaining icing over evenly.

Arrange the pecans all around the top outside edge of the sponge to decorate and then serve.

RIDICULOUSLY RICH CHOCOLATE TART

SERVES
8

This chocolate tart is so dark and rich, it is just not for kids! There is a little bit of faffing here, what with making the pastry and all that, but to cut a perfectly acceptable corner just buy ready-made sweet shortcrust pastry instead to halve the making time.

SHORTCRUST PASTRY
125g butter, softened and diced, plus extra for greasing
100g caster sugar
Pinch of salt (but only if your butter is unsalted)
250g plain flour, plus extra for dusting
1 egg, at room temperature

CHOCOLATE FILLING
100ml single or double cream
250ml whole milk
175g dark chocolate (minimum 70% cocoa solids)
75g milk chocolate
3 eggs
Finely grated zest of 1 large orange

EQUIPMENT
20cm straight-edged tart tin

Grease a 20cm straight-edged tart tin well with a little butter and set aside on a baking sheet.

I prefer to make this pastry using a food processor. Put the butter, sugar and salt in the processor and blitz for about 10 seconds. Then add the flour and pulse a few times until everything is nicely mixed up. Tip in the egg and pulse a few times again, scraping the sides of the food processor if need be. Lay a large piece of cling film on the work surface, tip the pastry mix on to it, squidge the pastry together in a ball and then wrap it up in the cling film. Place it in the fridge and leave it to rest for a good hour or hour and a half.

To make the pastry the traditional way by hand, tip the flour onto a clean work surface, then make a well in the centre of the flour about 30cm wide. Put the butter and the sugar and salt in the centre of the well (they should not touch the flour at this time). Use your hand to mix the butter, sugar and salt together; it is kind of messy, but great to make it the way it should be made! Then bring in the flour. I use a pastry scraper to flick the flour over the butter and the sugar, and then I kind of chop it together until it resembles fine breadcrumbs. Make another well in the centre of the pastry mix and crack the egg into it. Then, using your fingertips, mix it all together; again messy, but I find it kind of fun. Once the mixture is all mixed up and together, wrap the pastry ball in cling film and pop it in the fridge for an hour or hour and a half to rest. The pastry needs to rest to relax the protein strands, which could cause it to be too stretchy when you roll it. This will also help make the pastry more tender.

Once the pastry is rested, roll it out on a lightly floured surface to about a 25cm circle, roughly 5mm in thickness. I then put a rolling pin across the centre of the dough and flip half of the pastry over the rolling pin. Pick it up on the rolling pin and lay the pastry over the tart tin before removing the rolling pin. Gently press the pastry down into the tin, making sure that the pastry goes right into the 'corners', and then pop it in the fridge for an hour to rest again (rolling it out works the proteins in the pastry again, so it needs to have another rest in the fridge). ≫

RIDICULOUSLY RICH CHOCOLATE TART

(continued)

Once the pastry has been in the fridge for 40 minutes, turn the oven on to preheat to 200°C, (fan 180°C), 400°F, Gas Mark 6 with the middle shelf at the ready.

After the pastry case has had an hour in the fridge and the oven is ready, line it with a circle of baking parchment slightly larger than the size of the tart case and tip in ceramic baking beans (or you can use dried beans for this, which are cheaper and work really well). Bake in the oven for 20 minutes until crisp, golden and almost cooked through.

Meanwhile, to prepare the filling, put the cream and milk in a medium pan and bring it almost to the boil, then immediately remove it from the heat. Snap in the dark and milk chocolates and leave it aside to melt. Once the chocolate has softened and melted, mix it all together and add the eggs and the orange zest. Mix together again and then set this aside.

Remove the pastry case from the oven and leave the oven open to cool down a bit, turning the temperature down to 180°C, (fan 160°C), 350°F, Gas Mark 4.

Carefully lift the bean-filled baking parchment from the pastry case. Once the oven has reached temperature (which will be indicated by the thermostat light coming back on), close the door. Pour the chocolate mix into the pastry case. I like to pour the last bit of filling into the case once it is safely resting on the oven shelf, that way it avoids any spillover. Then very carefully place the pastry case back into the oven for 20–25 minutes.

Once baked, remove from the oven and leave to cool for a bit. Then carefully push the tart out of the tin, remove the base, place on a plate or cake stand and serve.

GHOSTLY BLACK-EYED MERINGUES

MAKES
12

I saw these many moons ago at a Halloween party in New York. The States do Halloween in a much bigger way than we do. You can also dress the ghosts up with those red shoe laces for hair, if you wish, for a ghostly and ghoulish 31st October!

225g caster sugar
4 egg whites
1 squeeze of lemon juice
   (about ½ tsp)

TO DECORATE
1 tsp black writing icing from a tube (I found it in the supermarket)
or 1 tsp melted chocolate in a small piping bag
or 15g black fondant icing, rolled into 24 tiny balls

Preheat the oven to 140°C, (fan 120°C), 275°F, Gas Mark 1. Line one large baking sheet with baking parchment.

An electric whisk or a freestanding electric mixer set with the whisk attachment is best for this, rather than doing it by hand. This is a backward way of making a meringue, but I find it works every time. Put the sugar, two of the egg whites and the lemon juice in a large bowl. Mix everything together on high for 2–3 minutes until thick and creamy.

Then add one more egg white and continue to whisk for 2–3 minutes more until it becomes stiff and shiny. Finally, add the last egg white and continue to whisk for about 3–4 minutes until the mixture is really, really stiff and holding peaks. To test if it is ready, take some egg white on the end of a whisk so the whisk is facing downwards and then turn the whisk so the handle is now down and the meringue is upright. The meringue should stand proud and not flop. If it does flop, then keep on whisking away until you get there for really stiff and shiny meringues.

Once the meringue mixture is ready, spoon it into a piping bag fitted with a 1cm nozzle. You may need to do this in two batches, depending on the size of your piping bag. Don't overfill the bag or it will squidge out of the top when piping. Holding the nozzle downwards and the piping bag straight up, squeeze out one meringue ghost. I like to pipe a small circle about 5cm wide and then do a spiral going upwards (to about 5cm in height) to give a ghost-like look! Or you can just pipe big splodges, making sure you get a peak on the top. Repeat to make twelve in total. Space them a little apart on the tray as they will spread a bit when cooking.

Bake in the oven for about 1–1¼ hours or until the meringue is crisp on the outside, but still a bit chewy and soft on the inside (which you can tell by gently pressing the bottoms). Some days the meringues have cooked in less than an hour for me, and then sometimes in well over an hour, so test them after about 50 minutes and see how they are. ≫

So much depends on the type of weather that we are having. If the weather is very humid and there is lots of moisture in the atmosphere, then they can take quite a while longer to cook. Once cooked, remove them from the oven and leave to cool completely.

Once cool, carefully pipe eyes near the tops of each ghostly meringue using the black icing or melted chocolate. If you are feeling really adventurous, you can pipe on a ghostly mouth too! Alternatively, gently press the black fondant icing balls onto the meringues to stick. Arrange on a cake stand or serving platter and serve.

LIGHTER CHOCOLATE MUFFIN SPIDERS

MAKES
12

275g self-raising flour
50g dark chocolate chips
50g caster sugar
25g cocoa powder, sifted
1 tsp baking powder
½ tsp bicarbonate of soda
1 egg
2 egg whites
275ml semi-skimmed milk
50ml sunflower oil
300g cream cheese
50g crème fraîche
3 tbsp icing sugar, sifted
Seeds of ½ a vanilla pod (or a
    couple of drops of vanilla extract)

TO DECORATE
50g strawberry or
    cola laces (sweets),
    cut into 96 x 5cm lengths
24 M&Ms or Smarties

EQUIPMENT
12-hole muffin tin with
    paper muffin cases

Using semi-skimmed milk and egg whites make these scary spiders a little less naughty than traditional muffins. There is often a lot of drudgery at various stages in our lives, so for me it is important to have fun wherever possible. So don't only make these cakes if you have kids – invite some friends around for Halloween (dress code: spooky!) and get baking.

Preheat the oven to 210°C, (fan 190°C), 410°F, Gas Mark 6½. Line a 12-hole muffin tin with paper muffin cases.

Put the flour, chocolate chips, sugar, cocoa powder, baking powder and bicarb into a medium bowl. Toss together briefly and make a well in the centre. Beat the egg and egg whites together briefly in a small bowl to combine and pour them into the centre of the dry ingredients. Add the milk and sunflower oil also and mix everything together until well combined and smooth.

Using two spoons, divide the mixture evenly among the paper cases. They should be filled just over halfway in the case. Bake in the oven for about 20 minutes or until a skewer inserted in the centre of a muffin comes out clean. Once cooked, remove from the oven and leave to cool.

Meanwhile, prepare the icing. Simply beat the cream cheese, crème fraîche, icing sugar and vanilla seeds (or extract) together in a medium bowl until smooth. Cover and leave in the fridge until ready to use.

Once cool, place the muffins onto a serving plate. Divide the icing among the twelve muffins and use a small palette knife or round-bladed knife to spread as evenly as possible over the top of each one. Stick one strawberry or cola lace piece into the icing, near the centre, and leave it hanging down so it reaches to the plate. Repeat to give four legs on each side of every cupcake.

Stick on the M&Ms or Smarties for the eyes just before serving (any earlier and they will bleed onto the icing).

S'MORES POPS

MAKES
20

I do not think that s'mores have the same resonance in the UK as they do in the USA. In fact, I am sure of it. But I would like to give them the Blighty welcome that they deserve. They are naughty, but taste like a little bit of sweet heaven on a stick. You can buy the lollipop sticks online or in some supermarkets.

20 regular-sized marshmallows (from a 180g bag)
100g dark chocolate (minimum 70% cocoa solids) or milk chocolate
50g digestive or ginger nut biscuits

EQUIPMENT
20 lollipop sticks

Line a baking sheet with parchment paper. Push the end of each lollipop stick into the marshmallows (into the narrower end if applicable), standing them on the tray as you go. Push the sticks quite far in, but you do not want them coming out the other side!

I like to toast the marshmallows over a gas flame (get an adult only to do this), until they are just starting to caramelise. Working with one at a time, swirl it about briefly over the flame, being careful not to let the stick catch fire. Return the pop to the tray as you go, without touching the mallow as its centre will be molten hot. Don't be tempted to lift it back up until set firm or the stick may pull out of its soft centre.

Meanwhile, break the chocolate into a small bowl and either melt sitting on top of a pan of simmering water (without allowing the bowl and water to touch) or in 30-second blasts in the microwave, stirring between each go. Once melted, stir until smooth and set aside to cool a little.

Pop the biscuits into a resealable food bag and bash them to fine crumbs with a rolling pin. Tip them into a small bowl.

Once the mallows are firm, holding the stick, dip one into the melted chocolate so it comes up about one-third of the height of the marshmallow. Tilting the bowl to pool the chocolate will help. Allow the excess chocolate to drip off and then immediately dip it into the biscuit mix, so it comes up to almost the top of the chocolate. Return the marshmallows to the tray as you coat them, repeating until all the ingredients have been used up. Eat straight away or set them aside for about 30 minutes if you prefer the chocolate to be set firm.

You can serve the pops propped up inside a glass, stick side down, or arrange them stick side up on a serving platter. Alternatively, you can just serve them unassembled for people to help themselves to and get stuck in!

TOFFEE APPLE SLICE POPS

MAKES
12–16

225g caster sugar
2 tbsp golden syrup
1 tsp lemon juice
3–4 Granny Smith or Golden Delicious apples, depending on size, well washed and dried

EQUIPMENT
12–16 lollipop sticks

Toffee apples remind me of autumn turning into winter. Bonfires, shorter days and longer nights. But the problem with toffee apples is that they are kind of tough to eat. And to be honest, I do struggle to eat a whole one. So I have shrunk down the need to eat a whole toffee apple with these dainty little slices.

Put the sugar and 50ml water into a small pan over a low to medium heat and cook for about 3 minutes until the sugar dissolves, stirring occasionally. Add the golden syrup and lemon juice (the juice is said to help prevent the caramel from forming a hard, sticky lump and caramelising during the cooking process). Leave the mixture to simmer for about 12–15 minutes. Avoid stirring the mixture as this may cause crystalisation, but instead swirl the mixture gently in the pan every so often. Be super, super careful whilst you are cooking it as, I am sure you know, hot sugar is so dangerous.

The caramel is ready when it reaches 150°C (hard crack stage) on a sugar thermometer. If you do not have a sugar thermometer, then the best way to test to see if it is ready is to very carefully take out a small bit of the caramel on a spoon, let the caramel slide into a glass of cold water and leave to firm up for a moment or two. When the caramel in the glass is cool, lift it out with a spoon and try to break it in half. It should snap, which is called the hard crack stage. It can take quite a while to reach this stage and so test the caramel every few minutes. It should be a good golden brown in colour.

While you are waiting for the temperature to be reached, line a large tray with baking parchment and set aside.

Once the sugar has reached hard crack stage, it should be a rich, dark brown colour (but not burnt!). Remove it from the heat and immediately dunk the base of the pan into a wide bowl of cold water (without allowing the water to flow into the toffee). This will instantly stop the mixture from cooking further and begin the cooling and thickening process. It needs to be slightly thick to coat the apples – not too thin where it flows off and not too thick where it sets in clumps. Leave it aside for a few minutes to cool and thicken to the perfect consistency. »

Meanwhile, cut the apples into quarters and remove the core. Slide a lollipop stick into each apple wedge, either through the length or across the width, without going the whole way through. Dab the cut edges of each apple piece really well with kitchen towel until completely dry. This is very important as any moisture from the apple will cause the toffee to slide off.

Working quickly and carefully (again without allowing the toffee to touch your skin) and holding the stick, dip the apple wedges, one at a time, into the toffee, twirling them around until completely coated. Tilting the pan to one side to make a pool of toffee will be helpful. Allow excess toffee to drip off before laying the apple wedges skin-side down on the paper-lined tray as you go. At this stage you could sprinkle some edible yummies like hundreds and thousands on them. Set them aside for about 20 minutes or until set hard. If the toffee becomes too thick to work with, then return it briefly to a low heat to melt and again cool it down in water, if necessary, to bring it back to the perfect consistency.

Carefully peel the set toffee apples from the paper, arrange them upright in glasses and serve at once. These may start to weep, which would cause the toffee to slip off, and so are not suitable to make in advance.

Top tip
Once you have made these caramelised lovelies, there will be some toffee left in the bottom of your pan. The best way to remove it is to cover the toffee with water, bring the pan to the boil until the toffee comes off, and then discard the water down the drain.

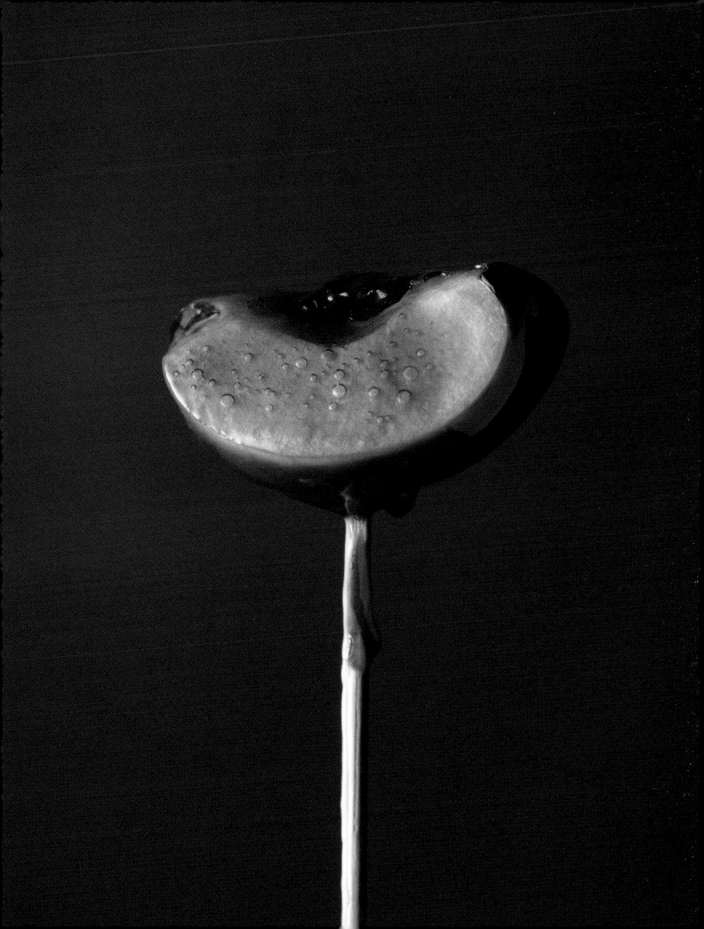

COCONUT KISSES WITH GINGER FILLY CHANTILLY AND STRAWBERRY SLICE

MAKES
24

100g desiccated coconut
200g caster sugar
4 egg whites

GINGER FILLY CHANTILLY
200g low-fat cream cheese
2½ tsp icing sugar
Seeds of 1 vanilla pod
2 knobs of stem ginger (from a jar
    in syrup), really finely diced, plus
    1 tbsp of the ginger syrup

8 medium-large strawberries,
    hulled, pointed ends trimmed and
    each one cut into three discs

I think these little kisses are just so cute and great for parties and special occasions. I simply love the colour red and the way it contrasts against the white ... anyway, I digress. I was making meringues one day and wondered what I had in my kitchen cupboard to make them a little more interesting. I came across chocolate, almonds and desiccated coconut and settled on using the latter. Once the coconut is roasted, it takes the edge off the sweetness, giving a much more mellow flavour, but still making these meringues really rather special.

Preheat the oven to 110°C (fan 90°C), 225°F, Gas Mark ¼. Line two large baking sheets with parchment paper and set aside. Heat a large frying pan (with no oil in it) over a medium heat and toast the coconut for a few minutes until golden brown. Tip into a bowl and set aside.

I have made meringues by hand, but it does take a very, very long time. So I prefer to use an electric mixer to do the job for me. Put the sugar and one of the egg whites into a clean bowl and mix for about 30 seconds on a high speed. Then add another egg white and whisk for about 2 minutes more. The mixture will start to become quite thick. Add the remaining egg whites, one at a time, beating well between each addition. Then whisk until the mixture is really stiff, white and shiny. It should become so stiff that if you turned the bowl upside down, the meringue would not come out! Finally, gently fold in the coconut until well combined.

Using a large spoon, scoop the mixture into a piping bag fitted with a 1.5cm plain nozzle. Pipe out 48 blobs, spaced apart on the baking sheets, with each one measuring 3–4cm wide and with a little Mr Whippy peak on the top (about 2cm in height). Pop them in the oven for around 1 hour 30 minutes or until the meringues are crisp on the outside, but still a little soft on the inside. Swap the trays around on the shelves halfway through the cooking time to ensure even cooking.

When the meringues are cooked, take them out of the oven and set aside to cool down. As they cool make the ginger filly Chantilly. Mix all of the ingredients together well and spoon it into a piping bag fitted with a 1.5cm plain nozzle. Pop into the fridge until ready to assemble.

Once the meringues are completely cool, pipe a small blob of the ginger filly on the bottom of two meringue pieces. Place a slice of strawberry on one of the filly Chantillys and then sandwich it together with the other Chantilly meringue. Repeat with the remaining meringues and filling to make 24 in total, arranging them on a large platter as you go. Serve straight away.

MINI WHITE CHOCOLATE NAPOLEONS WITH RASPBERRIES

MAKES
24

These are just so delicate and so pretty. I have made Napoleons/millefeuille using puff pastry and been happy with the results, but once in one of those indulgent pastry shops in Paris, I saw something similar but with layers of dark chocolate and vanilla pastry cream. Feel free to use light or dark chocolate in this recipe or mix up the layers of light and dark for extra dramatic effect. If you find your hands getting too warm as you assemble these, just pop your hands onto some frozen peas every now and again and then dry them off with a tea towel to keep your hands chocolatier cool.

CRÈME PÂTISSIÈRE
300ml milk
4 egg yolks
90g caster sugar
1 tbsp plain flour
1 tbsp cornflour
Seeds of 1 vanilla pod

CHOCOLATE LAYERS
400g milk, dark (minimum 70% cocoa solids) or white chocolate

TO DECORATE
24 raspberries
24 tiny fresh mint sprigs

First, make the crème pâtissière. Place the milk in a medium, wide pan on a medium heat and bring just to the boil. Meanwhile, beat together the egg yolks and sugar until combined. Then add the plain flour, cornflour and the vanilla seeds and beat until smooth and well blended. Remove the almost-boiling milk from the heat and pour half into the egg mixture while constantly whisking to avoid lumps. Pour this mixture into the remaining milk in the pan and return to a low heat. Whisk constantly until it returns to the boil, at which point it will be really thick and smooth. This should take about 6–8 minutes. Remove from the heat, press cling film down onto the surface to prevent a skin from forming and leave aside until cool. Then pop in the fridge until completely cold and really firm.

Meanwhile, prepare the chocolate layers. Cut out two 23 x 25cm pieces of baking parchment and sit each on a baking sheet. Break the chocolate into a medium bowl and either melt sitting on top of a pan of simmering water (without allowing the bowl and water to touch) or in 30-second blasts in the microwave, stirring between each go. Once melted, stir until smooth and divide it evenly between the centre of each piece of paper. Pop a tiny dot of melted chocolate under each corner of the papers to stick them to the baking sheets and prevent the paper from moving about. With a palette knife, spread the chocolate all over the papers, right out to the edges, in a smooth, even layer. Try to get the edges as straight as possible. Pop both in the fridge for 30 minutes or until set firm.

Once firm, remove the set chocolate from the fridge. Dip a long, sharp knife into really hot water and wipe dry. Run the knife under one of the pieces of paper to release it from the tray and then cut the chocolate into thirty-six 2.5 x 6cm rectangles. To do this, cut down the length into four 6cm wide strips and then across the width into nine 2.5cm wide pieces. Carefully peel each one from the baking parchment and lay on a clean board. Trim any ragged edges to neaten the rectangles up. Repeat with the second tray of set chocolate ≫

MINI WHITE CHOCOLATE NAPOLEONS WITH RASPBERRIES

(continued)

to give seventy-two rectangles in total. If they feel like they are getting too soft at any point, then return them to the fridge until hardened. Likewise, if they are shattering when being cut, it means they are too hard and brittle and so leave them to warm to room temperature before continuing. Any broken ones can be used in the middle of the stack later and nobody will know! Return the rectangles to the fridge until needed. Everything can be prepared to this point up to 24 hours in advance and then assembled just before serving.

Once cool, put the crème pâtissière into a piping bag fitted with a 2.5mm plain nozzle. If you have difficulty finding this size nozzle, then simply cut this size opening in a disposable piping bag. Lay out forty-eight of the chocolate rectangles and pipe the crème pâtissière onto these in three rows of seven tiny dots.

Carefully stack one of these rectangles on top of another and then top with one of the plain chocolate rectangles. There will be three layers of chocolate and two layers of the crème pâtissière.

To finish, pipe a small dot of the remaining crème pâtissière on the top centre of the Napoleon and sit a raspberry on top to stick. Decorate with a mint sprig and arrange on a serving platter or cake stand. Repeat with the remaining ingredients to make twenty-four in total. Serve at once.

Top tip
I know piping looks hard, but the trick is to hold the pipette vertically. Then it's easy.

GRANNY SMITH BIRCHER MUESLI

SERVES
6-8

200g porridge oats
300g Greek or natural yogurt,
    full- low- or no-fat
Seeds of 1 vanilla pod or a few
    drops of vanilla extract (optional)
3 Granny Smith apples, roughly
    grated to the core
100ml apple juice or water
1–2 tbsp maple syrup (optional)
1–2 tbsp honey (optional)

It is good to use a sour apple like the Granny Smith for this to counterbalance the sweetness of the maple syrup. This recipe can form a base Bircher muesli, which can be made with a variety of dried fruits and other breakfast yummies, such as toasted coconut or fresh fruit. Vanilla is the flavour queen for me in many sweet dishes and will give this muesli a nice edge, but the dish will taste delicious without it.

Mix the oats in a large bowl with the yogurt, vanilla (if using), apple and apple juice or water and mix everything together to give a soft dropping consistency.

Cover and leave to stand in the fridge for about 15 minutes before serving.

Spoon into serving bowls and then drizzle with a little of the maple syrup and honey, if using.

This will keep in the fridge for a few hours, but eventually the apples will make the whole thing look a terrible brown, so it's best eaten quite soon after making.

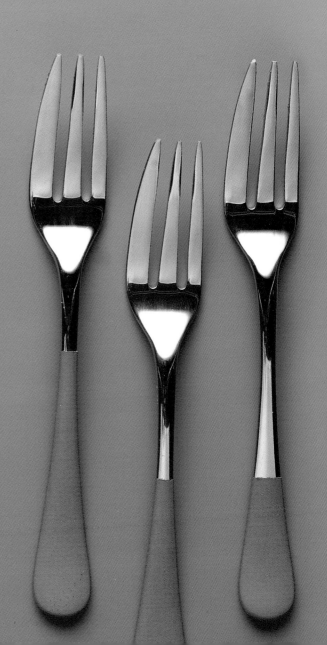

TIPS & TRICKS

I hope the recipes in this book have made you realise how easy cooking can be! So, in the spirit of keeping things simple, here are a few things that I've learned along the way that will help you hone your cooking skills and start to have even more fun in the kitchen.

I've made a list of all the storecupboard staples I've used in this book, and all the kit you need in your kitchen. And what could be better than recipes you can cook ahead for another day? I've made life easy here, too, and included some pointers on how to store food, or freeze it for the future, safely and with no wastage. And I've really embraced the slow cooker lifestyle! Bung everything in, turn it on and go about your business, and when you get home you have a delicious supper at the ready.

STORECUPBOARD ESSENTIALS

These are the ingredients I use most often in the recipes here and in my daily cooking – plus a few others for the more adventurous cook that you will become having read this book! Everything on this list can easily be bought in your local supermarket. Some things you'll use more often than others, some are essential, and some just add that extra zing. Get to know them, their flavours and textures, and give your food that wow factor.

SPICES:

- Cumin – ground and seed
- Coriander – ground and seed
- Paprika – regular and smoked
- Chilli powder – mild or hot, depending on your preference
- Cayenne pepper
- Turmeric
- Bay leaves
- Nutmeg
- Cardamom pods
- Cinnamon – ground and sticks
- Vanilla – extract and pods
- Cloves – ground and whole
- Allspice – ground and berries
- Mixed spice
- Ground ginger
- Chinese five-spice
- Szechuan peppercorns
- Curry powder – mild, medium or hot, depending on your preference
- Garam masala
- Sea salt and black peppercorns

BOTTLES AND CANS:

- Good-quality vegetable, chicken and beef stock
- Soy sauce
- Hoisin sauce
- Sesame oil
- Tomato purée
- Canned tomatoes – chopped are mostly used in this book
- Worcestershire sauce
- Ketchup
- Mustard – Dijon, English and wholegrain
- Coconut milk
- Sunflower oil – spray and liquid
- Olive oil
- Extra virgin olive oil
- Vinegar – red and white wine and cider
- Canned pulses – lentils and beans
- Capers

DRY GOODS:

- Sugar – caster and icing
- Soft brown sugar – light and dark
- Honey, golden syrup, treacle and molasses
- Flour – plain, wholemeal, self-raising and strong bread
- Baking powder
- Bicarbonate of soda
- Dried yeast – fast-action or easy blend
- Almonds – flaked, whole and ground
- Hazelnuts – blanched are more useful
- Pistachios
- Pine kernels
- Cashews – unsalted
- Peanuts – plain and roasted
- Pecans
- Walnuts
- Sesame seeds
- Raisins
- Sultanas
- Apricots
- Desiccated coconut
- Good-quality food colouring pastes
- Pasta
- Rice – white and brown
- Quinoa

KITCHEN ESSENTIALS

Get your kit together! This is my ultimate list of tools and gadgets that I swear by and I believe that every new cook needs in their kitchen. Again, some are vital and you can't cook without them, while a few are helpful corner-cutters that take the effort out of food preparation. Aim to have a good selection of these, but obviously keep in mind your cupboard space – don't go crazy if you don't have the storage!

- A selection of sturdy chopping boards – I keep one for veg, one for fruit or sweet things and another for meat and fish
- Good knives
- Selection of saucepans
- Casserole dish with lid
- Vegetable peeler for all of those carrot salads
- Selection of wooden spoons
- Large metal spoons, including a slotted one
- Fish slice
- Palette knife
- Pastry brush
- Scissors – especially a large pair for spatchcocking poultry
- Kitchen string
- Whisks in a variety of sizes
- Rolling pin
- Pastry cutters
- Baking sheets
- Roasting tins
- Cake tins – round, square and tray bake
- Small cake tins – cupcake and muffin
- Tart tins – fluted and plain
- Measuring jug
- Scales – preferably digital
- Hand-held mixer or free-standing mixer
- Food processor or mini whizzer
- Stick (or immersion) blender
- Colander
- Sieve
- Measuring spoons
- Grater

STORAGE AND FREEZING

The most delicious dishes rely on the best-quality ingredients, so you need to look after them if you want to get maximum flavour. Dried, fresh or frozen, there are ways in which you can keep these ingredients at their best, ready for whenever you need them. Follow these tips, and remember vigilance is key – always keep an eye on those use-by dates!

KEEPING YOUR FRUIT AND VEG FRESH:

The best way to ensure that you are cooking with and eating the freshest fruit and veggies is to buy only what you'll need for a few days at a time. Store soft fruits, such as berries, in the fridge but bring to room temperature to serve. Most other fruits can be stored in a fruit bowl in a cool spot in your kitchen and out of direct sunlight – unless you're ripening underripe fruit. Onions, garlic, potatoes and squash are best stored in a vegetable basket at room temperature out of direct sunlight and preferably in a darker corner. Most other veggies should be stored in the fridge in the salad crisper.

HOW TO STORE DRY SPICES

Dry spices are storecupboard essentials in my kitchen and I like to keep a varied selection, but they do have a shelf life and lose potency over time. Buying spices in bulk – although significantly cheaper than buying small jars – can be a false economy unless you plan to use them within a year. Ground spices are best used within one year and whole seeds such as cumin, coriander and cardamom will keep for longer – up to 3 years. Store spices in airtight jars, plastic food boxes or tins away from direct sunlight and heat, as heat and light will affect their strength and flavour.

FREEZING TIPS

To make the most use of your freezer you should always ensure that everything is clearly labelled with contents and the date of freezing. Bread, meat and fish all freeze very well and are useful to have on standby. Some raw fruits, such as berries, also fare well in the freezer – freeze them open on trays for 1 hour until solid and then pack into bags for storage. This will help to stop them going

mushy. Cooked fruit purées and soups of all kinds are brilliant freezer staples. Most foods will keep well in the freezer for up to 3 months. Supermarket packed meat and fish should be frozen in unopened packs and on the day of purchase. They will already be clearly marked with dates and contents, making identification easy at a later date. Cooked food should be completely cold before freezing and stored in either plastic food-safe freezer boxes or packed into secure freezer bags.

All meat and fish, whether raw or cooked, should be defrosted slowly in the fridge and cooked or eaten soon after defrosting. And never refrozen.

HOW TO LOOK AFTER YOUR KNIVES

All chefs bang on about knives, and rightly so. A strong, sharp knife is your friend in the kitchen and will make preparation so much easier. You don't have to buy expensive ones from Japan, but do try to buy the best you can afford; if you follow my few simple rules you can keep them in tip-top condition and you won't need to replace them for a long time.

To ensure that your knives are always in the best condition you should sharpen them before each and every use – either using a steel or sharpening stone – whichever you find easiest. After use, wash knives in hot soapy water and dry thoroughly before storing in either a wooden knife block, canvas roll or on a wall-mounted magnetic strip. Never store knives in a kitchen drawer jumbled with your other tools and kitchen equipment. This is not only dangerous, but can damage the blades

And there you have it – loads of simple, stunning recipes to suit every palate and every occasion and which will set you off and move you on in your culinary journey. Armed with these, a satisfyingly well-stocked storecupboard and all the kit you could possibly need, creating delicious dishes from scratch has become a doddle. So get in the kitchen, get cooking and enjoy!

INDEX

ACKNOWLEDGEMENTS

Acknowledgements are always the tricky part for me, as there are so many people to thank and I live in fear that I've forgotten someone! So first off, I'd love to thank my readers and followers – you guys are amazing – sending me photos of your finished dishes and always pitching in with an opinion or three when I'm torn between two ingredients to go into a dish (or which shoes to buy!). Thanks to all of you on Instagram, Facebook and Twitter for your support.

I also want to offer my deepest thanks to the team at James Grant who continue to be there for me day in and day out: Nicola Ibison, Mary Bekhait, Eugenie Furniss, Neil Rodford, Paul Worsley, Darren Worsley, Amy Newman, Sarah Hart, Karen Mills, Leon Harlow, Georgie White, Blaise McGowan and Riz Mansor.

Alison Kirkham and Janice Hadlow have been unwavering in their support for me at the BBC. Thank you for continuing to believe in me and giving me this incredible platform to do what I love to do!

Pete Lawrence (Executive Producer), Catherine Welton (Executive Producer), Jen Fazey (Series Producer), Sophia Reed (Assistant Producer), Susie Povey (Assistant Producer), Michelle Sodani (Production Manager), Lucy Marshall (Production Manager), Sarah Cole (Production Coordinator), Marianne Thomas (Studio Assistant), Wendy McCabe (Production Executive), Simon Weekes (Camera), Luke Cardiff (Camera), Dave Miller (Camera), Bill Rudolph, Tyrone Morgan (Camera assistant), Paul Allen (Lighting), Katy Roberts (Researcher), Emma Young (set dresser), Gary Skipton, Angela Maddick, Andy Sutton (the editors) and the brilliant director, Ed St Giles – thank you all for helping to create a series I am so proud of.

The excellent Michaela Bowles and her fantastic team Phil Wells and Rob Allison.

The wonderful Sharon Hearne-Smith for checking my recipes with such attention to detail, as always.

The team at HarperCollins and those on the shoot: Carole Tonkinson, Charlie Redmayne, Kate Elton, Natalie Jerome, Martin Topping, Georgina MacKenzie, Sim Greenaway, Maja Smend, Sam Folan, Annie Rigg, Kathryn Morrissey, Laura Rogers, Tony Hutchinson, Julie MacBrayne, Laura Lees and Orlando Mowbray.

Carlos Ferraz for his magic hands styling me for the book with hair and make-up.

Huge thanks to my wonderful publicist, Max Dundas as well as Nancy Sanders and the wider team at Dundas Communications, who have been fantastic throughout.

So much love goes out to my lovely family, who have been there constantly since the very beginning and continue to support me: Mum, Dad, Jace, Kate, Fran, Rachel, Auntie Angela, Victoria, James and my wonderful daughter Ella.

Rodney, Tony Walker, Velm, Jusy Joo, Lia Peralta, Maggie Draycott, Norie Lagmay, Keith Stoll, Satya and all my friends who have been a constant support – at all hours!

And as always I would like to mention the charities that I support: TACT care, Rays of Sunshine, The Princes Trust, Barnardos, Sutton Community Farm, The British Association for Adoption and Fostering and the Tope Foundation. I hope your stellar work continues and thank you for letting me be part of your success.